BestMasters

Mit **„BestMasters“** zeichnet Springer die besten Masterarbeiten aus, die an renommierten Hochschulen in Deutschland, Österreich und der Schweiz entstanden sind. Die mit Höchstnote ausgezeichneten Arbeiten wurden durch Gutachter zur Veröffentlichung empfohlen und behandeln aktuelle Themen aus unterschiedlichen Fachgebieten der Naturwissenschaften, Psychologie, Technik und Wirtschaftswissenschaften. Die Reihe wendet sich an Praktiker und Wissenschaftler gleichermaßen und soll insbesondere auch Nachwuchswissenschaftlern Orientierung geben.

Springer awards **“BestMasters”** to the best master’s theses which have been completed at renowned Universities in Germany, Austria, and Switzerland. The studies received highest marks and were recommended for publication by supervisors. They address current issues from various fields of research in natural sciences, psychology, technology, and economics. The series addresses practitioners as well as scientists and, in particular, offers guidance for early stage researchers.

Carolin Seibert

Differences between FIN 48 and IFRIC 23

A Critical Analysis

Springer Gabler

Carolin Seibert
Bonn, Germany

ISSN 2625-3577 ISSN 2625-3615 (electronic)
BestMasters
ISBN 978-3-658-39040-2 ISBN 978-3-658-39041-9 (eBook)
https://doi.org/10.1007/978-3-658-39041-9

Responsible Editor: Marija Kojic
This Springer Gabler imprint is published by the registered company Springer Fachmedien Wiesbaden GmbH, part of Springer Nature.
The registered company address is: Abraham-Lincoln-Str. 46, 65189 Wiesbaden, Germany

Contents

Abbreviations

ACCA	Association of Chartered Certified Accountants
AcSEC	Accounting Standards Executive Committee
AEAO	Anwendungserlass zur Abgabenordnung (German Fiscal Code Application Decree)
AICPA	American Institute of Certified Public Accountants
AO	Abgabenordnung (German Fiscal Code)
APA	Advance Pricing Agreement
App.	Appendix
Art.	Article
ASC	Accounting Standards Codification
AStG	Außensteuergesetz (German Foreign Tax Act)
BaFin	Bundesanstalt für Finanzdienstleistungsaufsicht (German Federal Financial Supervisory Authority)
BB	Der Betriebs-Berater (German journal for business administration and business law)
BB&T	Branch Banking and Trust
BEA	Bureau of Economic Analysis
BFH	Bundesfinanzhof (German Federal Fiscal Court)
BFuP	Betriebswirtschaftliche Forschung und Praxis (German journal for business research and practice)
BMF	Bundesministerium für Finanzen (German Federal Ministry of Finance)
CAP	Compliance Assurance Process
CEO	Chief Executive Officer
CRSP	Center for Research in Security Prices
CSR	Corporate Social Responsibility

CU	currency unit
DAX	Deutscher Aktien Index (German stock index)
DB	Der Betrieb (German journal for business administration, tax law, commercial law and labor law)
DRSC	Deutsche Rechnungslegungs Standards Committee (Accounting Standards Committee of Germany)
DStR	Deutsches Steuerrecht (German journal for German tax law)
e.g.	exampli gratia (for example)
EC	European Community
ED	Exposure Draft
EDGAR	Electronic Data Gathering, Analysis, and Retrieval
EEC	European Economic Community
EFRAG	European Financial Reporting Advisory Group
ESMA	European Securities and Markets Authority
et al.	et alii (and others)
et seq.	et sequens (and the following recital or page)
et seqq.	et sequentes (and the following recitals or pages)
etc.	et cetera (and so on)
ETPF	European Tax Policy Forum
ETR	effective tax rate
EU	European Union
EY	Ernst & Young
FAF	Financial Accounting Foundation
FAS	Financial Accounting Standards
FASB	Financial Accounting Standards Board
FEI	Financial Executives International
FGO	Finanzgerichtsordnung (German Code of Administrative Court Procedure)
Fig.	Figure
FIN 48	FASB Interpretation 48
FREP	Financial Reporting Enforcement Panel
G20	Group of Twenty
GAAP	Generally Accepted Accounting Principles
GmbHR	Die GmbH-Rundschau (German journal for limited liability companies)
HGB	Handelsgesetzbuch (German Commercial Code)
i.e.	id est (that means)
I/B/E/S	Institutional Brokers' Estimate System
IAS	International Accounting Standards

IASB	International Accounting Standards Board
ICAP	International Compliance Assurance Programme
IESBA	International Ethics Standards Board for Accountants
IFRIC 23	IASB Interpretation 23
IFRS	International Financial Reporting Standard
IFRS IC	International Financial Reporting Standards Interpretations Committee
IRS	Internal Revenue Service
IRZ	Zeitschrift für Internationale Rechnungslegung (German journal for international accounting)
IStR	Internationales Steuerrecht (German journal for international tax law)
IT	information technology
IWB	Internationale Wirtschaftsbriefe (German journal for tax law and business law)
KoR	Zeitschrift für internationale und kapitalmarktorientierte Rechnungslegung (German journal for capital market oriented and international accounting)
KStG	Körperschaftsteuergesetz (German Corporation Tax Act)
LB&I	Large Business and International
MDAX	Mid-Cap Deutscher Aktien Index (Mid-Cap German stock index)
NIFRIC	Non-IASB Interpretation
No.	Number
NRW	North Rhine-Westphalia
OECD	Organisation for Economic Co-operation and Development
OTSA	Office of Tax Shelter Analysis Application
p.	page
Para.	Paragraph
PATA	Pacific Asia Travel Association
PiR	Praxis der internationalen Rechnungslegung (German journal for international accounting practice)
pp.	pages
PwC	PricewaterhouseCoopers
rec.	recital
S&P	Standard and Poor's
SAB	Staff Accounting Bulletin
SEC	United States Securities and Exchange Commission
Sec.	Section
SFAS	Statement of Financial Accounting Standards

SOX	Sarbanes-Oxley Act
Stbg	Die Steuerberatung (German journal for tax advice)
StBp	Die steuerliche Betriebsprüfung (German journal for tax audits)
SteuK	Steuerrecht kurzgefaßt (German journal for tax law)
StuW	Steuer und Wirtschaft (German journal for tax law)
Tab.	Table
TEI	Tax Executives Institute
Ubg	Die Unternehmensbesteuerung (German journal for corporate taxation)
US	United States
US GAAP	United States Generally Accepted Accounting Principles
USA	United States of America
USD	United States dollar
UTB	unrecognized tax benefit
UTP	uncertain tax position
VHB	Verband der Hochschullehrer für Betriebswirtschaft (German Academic Association of Business Research)
Vol.	Volume
WPg	Die Wirtschaftsprüfung (German journal for auditing)

1 Introduction

Tax uncertainty is extremely high and continues to grow (ETPF, 2020, p. 15). This is the conclusion of a cross-country survey conducted by the European Tax Policy Forum (ETPF) at different intervals between January 2016 and October 2020 and was presented at the Joint Conference of the ETPF and the Tax Foundation on November 2, 2020 (ETPF, 2020, p. 1). Respondents experienced the complexity in the tax code, frequent changes in the statutory tax system and unpredictable or inconsistent treatments by tax authorities as the top three sources of tax uncertainty (ETPF, 2020, p. 8). Despite the ambiguous legal situation, tax rules must be interpreted as part of the declaration process and a specific tax position must be taken in the tax return. The final tax assessment, however, is usually made after the conclusion of a tax audit or the termination of a legal proceeding (Suermann, Kämpfer and Müller, 2016, p. 415). From an accounting point of view, when preparing annual financial statements, it is therefore never known whether the tax charge corresponding to the declaration and entered in the annual financial statement is correct and final (Hoffmann, 2010, p. 238). The lack of specific IFRS rules for the accounting for these uncertain tax positions allowed IFRS reporters a high degree of flexibility in accounting which led to the establishment of different practices (IASB, 2017, p. 5). Due to the lack of regulations in IFRS, many companies have relied on the US regulations for accounting for uncertain tax positions codified in FIN 48 (Loitz, 2017, p. M5). With the enactment of IFRIC 23, this legal loophole has been closed now.

In light of the first-time application of IFRIC 23 for fiscal years beginning on or after January 1, 2019 (IASB, 2017, rec. B1), companies had to reassess their current accounting practice for uncertain tax positions. The new regulation has led to important changes, especially for German companies. According to the previous legal situation, German companies had to recognize but not to disclose provisions for uncertain tax positions (Hoffmann, 2010, p. 240). With IFRIC 23,

C. Seibert, *Differences between FIN 48 and IFRIC 23*, BestMasters,
https://doi.org/10.1007/978-3-658-39041-9_1

German companies have to report them in the same way as US companies (IASB, 2017, rec. BC22). Despite the harmonization efforts of FASB and IASB, full convergence often cannot be achieved. For companies that previously followed the provisions of FIN 48 or for companies that report their financial statements in accordance with both US GAAP and IFRS, it is therefore of particular importance to understand the differences between the two regulations.

The proper application of FIN 48 and IFRIC 23 is a highly debated topic in science and practice. The high number of 116 comment letters on FIN 48 (FASB, 2005, p. 1) and 61 comment letters on IFRIC 23 (IASB, 2016, p. 4) shows not only the practical importance of these regulations, but also the considerable problems associated with their applications. While the application of the respective standards is discussed frequently and extensively in literature, the differences between the two regulations are only rarely discussed (Penatzer, 2018, p. 777). Moreover, normative tax literature emphasizes the need for further discussion on this topic (Prinz, 2021, p. 9). Therefore, the objective of this thesis is to identify and analyze the differences between FIN 48 and IFRIC 23 as well as the practical implications of the newly introduced IFRIC 23 regulation.

To approach this objective, the thesis is divided into three sections. The theoretical part presented in Chapter 2 first provides an understanding of uncertain tax positions and then introduces the accounting regulations for uncertain tax positions according to FIN 48 and IFRIC 23. After presenting the respective legal provisions, empirical literature reviews are given in order to reflect the current state of research. Chapter 3 compares the two accounting standards on the basis of the previously presented accounting requirements. The differences identified are assessed critically with regard to their theoretical concepts and practical implications. Chapter 4 then analyzes the application difficulties that have arisen with the newly introduced IFRIC 23 from the perspective of different parties. For this purpose, five qualitative interviews were conducted: one with the German tax authority, two with the German business practice and two with the German advisory practice. Based on the previous analysis results and the empirical studies on FIN 48, three interview guides were created which consist of 37 questions each and are divided into the areas of general questions about IFRIC 23, specific questions about the challenges associated with the application of IFRIC 23 and possible solutions as well as questions about the impact of IFRIC 23 on tax avoidance and earnings management. The findings from the interviews are preceded by an analysis of the 2019 tax audit, an analysis of the effect of the first-time application of IFRIC 23 on 2019 consolidated financial statements and an analysis of the 2020 audit. The thesis concludes with a summary and reflection of the analysis results and provides an outlook on further research needs.

Conceptual Basis for Accounting for Uncertain Tax Positions 2

2.1 Significance of Uncertainties in Income Taxes for Tax Accounting

A uniform definition of uncertain tax positions has not been established in tax literature yet (Ludenia, 2006, p. 4). However, the definitions found reach a consensus with the following formulation: uncertain tax positions are liabilities (assets) that arise legally or economically on the balance sheet date and will lead to an outflow of funds (inflow of funds) in the future with a sufficient degree of probability, although their due date and amount are uncertain (Schlager, 1979, p. 336; Wacker, 1981, p. 259; Schramm, 1989, p. 8; Rose, 1995, p. 482; Hey, 2002, p. 64; Kröner and Beckenhaub, 2008, p. 130; Risse, 2012, p. 170).

Uncertain tax liabilities and assets are distributed differently over the taxation process (Simlacher, 2015, p. 2830). In order to determine the taxable income, entities have to prepare a tax return and submit it to the tax authorities. In doing so, they often have to make subjective assumptions about the tax treatment of business transactions (Herzig, Heimig and Vossel, 2009, p. 2613). Reasons for this are, for example, legal loopholes or different appraisals of tax situations (Hoffmann, 2010, p. 238). This leads to uncertainties regarding the actual tax burden. In addition, the income tax assessment can be subject to review by a later tax audit according to Sec. 164 of the German Fiscal Code (AO) or the tax assessment is provisional according to Sec. 165 AO. Moreover, tax assessments can be changed retrospectively according to Sec. 129, 130 et seq. and 172 et seqq. AO (Warsönke, 2020, p. 17). As a result, even after the tax return has been

Supplementary Information The online version contains supplementary material available at https://doi.org/10.1007/978-3-658-39041-9_2.

C. Seibert, *Differences between FIN 48 and IFRIC 23*, BestMasters,
https://doi.org/10.1007/978-3-658-39041-9_2

prepared and submitted, there is still uncertainty as to whether the actual tax burden deviates from the declared tax burden (Herzig, Heimig and Vossel, 2009, p. 2613). Only when the assessment period has expired within the meaning of Sec. 169 AO or the tax audit has been completed, there is certainty about the type and amount of tax consequences (Kämpfer, 2017, p. 454). At this stage of the taxation process, the reassessed tax liability can be higher than the declared tax liability. Thus, uncertain tax liabilities arise (Zwirner and Busch, 2016, p. 105). If a legal remedy procedure according to Sec. 347 et seqq. AO or a tax jurisdiction proceeding according to Sec. 33 et seqq. of the German Code of Administrative Court Procedure (FGO) is initiated and the taxpayer can expect to win, uncertain tax assets arise (Zwirner and Busch, 2016, p. 105).

Different types of uncertainty can occur in assessing taxes. Domestic issues often lead to disputes with tax authorities over tax-exempt business income and non-deductible business expenses (Simlacher, 2015, p. 2831). For example, costs incurred in the disposal of shares in a corporation might not be recognized by the tax authority as deductible operating expenses, but instead classified as disposal costs which would lead to a reduction in tax-free capital gain within the meaning of Sec. 8b Para. 2 Sentence 2 of the German Corporation Tax Act (KStG) (BMF, 2015, p. 612). This risk must be reflected by recognizing an uncertain tax liability (Simlacher, 2015, p. 2831).

When it comes to cross-border issues, transfer pricing structures often lead to uncertain tax positions (Mammen, 2011, p. 503). Transfer prices, agreed in intra-group deliveries between a German parent company and a foreign subsidiary, which violate the arm's length principle within the meaning of Sec. 1 Para. 1 Sentence 1 of the German Foreign Tax Act (AStG) result in an off-balance-sheet increase in profit for the parent company and thus in an additional tax payment. Therefore, an uncertain tax liability has to be recognized (Simlacher, 2015, p. 2832). It is questionable whether the subsidiary can recognize a corresponding tax asset (Frink, 2015, p. 9). In principle, this is only possible if there is a double tax treaty with mutual agreement procedure and the obligation to initiate arbitration proceedings between the states according to Art. 25 Para. 1, 2 and 5 of the OECD Model Tax Convention (Frink, 2015, p. 9). The absence of an arbitration clause leads to the recognition of an uncertain tax asset (Flüchter, 2012, p. 695).

In addition to the accounting for current taxes, tax uncertainties can also affect deferred taxes. For example, different views between taxpayers and tax authorities about the tax depreciation period of an asset lead to uncertain tax positions and adjustments of deferred taxes (Jacob and Kazuch, 2018, p. 208).

It remains to be emphasized that uncertain tax liabilities and assets have a significant impact on tax accounting. In particular, because the amounts deferred are often very high due to the long period between financial statements and tax audit reports, which is between five and eight years for most industrial countries (Kröner and Beckenhaub, 2008, p. 130). This raises the question of how these uncertainties have to be addressed in US GAAP and IFRS financial statements.

2.2 Accounting for Uncertain Tax Positions under FIN 48

2.2.1 Background

For US GAAP reporters, accounting for uncertain tax positions is regulated in FIN 48, which is an interpretation of FASB Statement No. 109, Accounting for Income Taxes, and was published on July 13, 2006 (FASB, 2006, p. 1). On July 1, 2009, all US GAAP accounting regulations were combined in a new set of rules, so that FIN 48 is now codified in ASC 740–10 (FASB, 2009, p. 10). In the following, the terminology of the previously known FIN 48 regulation is used.

Prior to the issuance of FIN 48, FASB Statement No. 5, Accounting for Contingencies, was used to account for uncertain tax positions (AICPA, 2006, p. 3). However, this regulation did not contain specific rules on accounting for potential tax contingencies, so that diverse practices have been applied (Browne, 2005, p. 975). While some entities only recorded accruals for tax contingencies that met the recognition threshold, others recorded accruals for each identified uncertain tax position at the expected amount (Deloitte, 2007, p. 2). By the recognition and reversal of accruals, entities could affect their annual net profit and pursue earnings management (Holzmann and Robinson, 2007, p. 88). This diversity in practice prompted the FASB to introduce FIN 48 (Kloosterhof and van Zoelen, 2009, p. 4). The objective of FIN 48 is to restrict the existing accounting options and discretions as well as to standardize accounting practice in order to improve the comparability of financial statements (FASB, 2006, rec. 2).

2.2.2 Scope

The application of FIN 48 is mandatory for all US GAAP reporting entities that are potentially subject to income taxes, regardless of whether they are currently subject to an income tax exemption, only receive tax-free income or are considered as fiscally transparent (FASB, 2006, rec. 1; Siegel, 2008, p. 2).

The regulations in FIN 48 are to be applied to all fiscal years beginning after December 15, 2006 (FASB, 2006, rec. 22). An earlier application was permitted if the entity did not issue interim financial statements in the period FIN 48 was adopted (Epstein, Nach and Bragg, 2007, p. 898). The cumulative effect of adopting FIN 48 was recognized as an adjustment to the opening balance of retained earnings (FASB, 2006, rec. B72; AICPA, 2006, p. 7).

FIN 48 is applicable to all tax positions within the scope of FASB Statement No. 109 (FASB, 2006, rec. 3). These contain all domestic and foreign federal, state and local income taxes (FASB, 1992, p. 7). Non-income-based taxes or levies are not covered by FIN 48 and should therefore be accounted for under FASB Statement No. 5 (Deloitte, 2007, p. 4). FIN 48 applies to tax positions that have been taken previously or are expected to be taken by an entity in its tax returns with regard to both current and deferred taxes (FASB, 2006, rec. 4).

Income tax uncertainties existing or arising at the time of a business combination are also within the scope of FIN 48 (FASB, 2006, rec. B10). The recognition and measurement criteria in FIN 48 apply to both the acquired current as well as deferred tax assets and liabilities (FASB, 2006, rec. C4). Moreover, FIN 48 provides guidance on the accounting for interest and penalties associated with uncertain tax positions (FASB, 2006, rec. 15 et seq.).

2.2.3 Recognition

After identifying all relevant uncertainties for all open tax years and jurisdictions, the appropriate unit of account must be determined (Deloitte, 2007, p. 9). This is important as the degree of aggregation can have an impact on reaching the recognition threshold (Cohen and Micheluzzi, 2006, p. 234). With a high degree, tax positions could be taken into account that show a low level of uncertainty and, viewed in isolation, would not lead to an adjustment of the declared tax liability (Sharma and Eberle, 2007, p. 32). Tax positions can be evaluated at the transaction level, tax return line item level or a subset thereof (Deloitte, 2007, p. 11). FIN 48 does not prescribe a unit of account to be used. However, it indicates that the determination is based on the manner in which the entity prepares its tax return and the audit approach that tax authorities are likely to pursue in a tax audit (FASB, 2006, rec. 5). A high degree of aggregation is recommended if there are interdependencies between business transactions, e.g., in the case of group transfer prices if a mutual agreement or arbitration procedure is applied (Donohue, Lowell and Martin, 2007, p. 487). However, business transactions must be considered individually if, e.g., the tax deductibility of an expense item is disputed (Andreoli, Colker and Lebovitz, 2007, p. 45). Once the unit of account is determined, each tax position is evaluated independently without the possibility of aggregation or offset with other positions (FASB, 2006, rec. 7c).

Both in assessing the recognition threshold and the subsequent measurement, an entity must assume that the tax authority will examine every tax position and has full knowledge and access to all relevant information (FASB, 2006, rec. B14). In addition, disputes will be taken to the court of last resort (FASB, 2006, rec. A3). Therefore, the detection risk is not considered (Dahlke, 2007, p. 313).

An entity must recognize a tax benefit of an uncertain tax position when the position reported on the tax return is more likely than not to be sustained upon examination by the tax authority, including appeals and litigation (FASB, 2006, rec. 6). The more-likely-than-not threshold is based on a likelihood greater than 50 percent (FASB, 2006, rec. 6). In performing this evaluation, technical merits of a position are taken into account (FASB, 2006, rec. 6). They are based on the application of sources of tax authorities and rely on generally accepted administrative practices and precedents of tax authorities in dealing with similar businesses (FASB, 2006, rec. 7b). However, negotiations with tax authorities are not considered (Donohue et al., 2007, p. 485). In assessing the recognition threshold, tax positions can be divided into three categories: The first category consists of positions that meet the recognition threshold and are highly certain to be sustained (Hennig, Raabe and Everett, 2008, p. 30). Based on clear and unambiguous tax law or a prior tax treatment that has been accepted by the tax authority, the entity can assume that the benefit will definitely be sustained. In this case, 100 percent of the benefit is recognized. The second category are positions that meet the recognition threshold but are not highly certain to be sustained (Kimmelfield, Horowitz and Davis, 2006, p. 294). The position has a likelihood of more than 50 percent but not 100 percent of being sustained. The amount of the tax benefit recognized is determined in the subsequent measurement step. The third category includes positions that do not meet the recognition threshold (Raby and Raby, 2006, p. 38). For these positions, no tax benefit is recognized.

2.2.4 Measurement

If a tax position meets the more-likely-than-not recognition threshold, but the full amount of the tax benefit is not highly certain of being sustained, the amount of the benefit recognized has to be measured (Garofalo and Valente, 2007, p. 49). The tax benefit is measured with the largest amount that has a cumulative probability of occurring of more than 50 percent (FASB, 2006, rec. 8). To do this, all possible outcomes of the tax benefits have to be estimated at first (FASB, 2006, rec. A21). Then, the probability of occurring is assigned to each outcome. The outcomes are sorted in descending order according to the amount. Afterwards, the individual probabilities of occurring are cumulated (FASB, 2006, rec. A22). The largest amount of the tax benefit that has a cumulative probability of occurring greater than 50 percent has to be recognized by the entity. A negative tax benefit cannot arise and the upper limit of a tax benefit is the tax benefit resulting from the tax return (Dahlke, 2007, p. 313). The evaluation should not only be based on the technical merits of the tax position, but on all relevant facts, circumstances and information available at the reporting date (FASB, 2006, rec. 8). Therefore, possible results of negotiations with tax authorities have to be included (Alltizer, McAllister and Jarnagin, 2008, p. 46).

At the end of each reporting period, all tax positions must be reevaluated based on new facts and circumstances regarding their recognition and measurement (FASB, 2006, rec. 12). A tax benefit that was initially not recognized but now meets the recognition criteria must be recognized (FASB, 2006, rec. 10). Accordingly, a previously recognized tax benefit that no longer meets the recognition criteria must be derecognized (FASB, 2006, rec. 11). In addition, a remeasurement is required if new information changes the computation of the recognized amount (Kimmelfield et al., 2006, p. 296). The adjustments must be made in the period in which the change in circumstances occurs (Sellner, 2006, p. 116).

2.2.5 Presentation and Disclosure

Due to the application of FIN 48, the amount of tax benefit recognized in the financial statement may differ from the amount taken or expected to be taken in the current year's tax return (Silliman and Fitzsimons, 2007, p. 42). This difference arises if less than 100 percent of the tax benefit is recognized, i.e., a tax position meets the recognition threshold but is not highly certain to be sustained or a tax position does not meet the recognition threshold. For the amount of the unrecognized tax benefit a liability must be recognized (FASB, 2006, rec. 17). If the liability is anticipated to be settled within one year, the liability is classified as current (FASB, 2006, rec. 17). Otherwise, it is classified as non-current. If the liability arises from taxable temporary differences, a deferred tax liability must be recognized which is to be classified as non-current (FASB, 2006, rec. 18).

Under FIN 48, there are specific disclosure requirements for unrecognized tax benefits (Brazzil and Stein, 2007, p. 566). Entities are required to disclose a tabular rollforward, the amounts affecting the effective tax rate, the interest and penalties, the amounts that are likely to materially change in the next 12 months, and a list of open tax years by major jurisdictions (FASB, 2006, rec. 21).

A summarizing illustration of the accounting regulations under FIN 48 and the individual steps for their implementation can be found in Appendix A.

2.2.6 Empirical Insights

The implementation of FIN 48 has led to the development of a series of empirical papers examining the determinants and implications of FIN 48. Appendix B provides a comprehensive overview of the existing empirical literature.

The manifold research results can be summarized in three main statements. First, research finds no support for firms' initial concern that the FIN 48 disclosure requirements increase their tax costs by providing the IRS a roadmap for auditing purposes (e.g., Frischmann et al., 2008, pp. 261–278). Second, the literature is inconclusive regarding the informativeness and usefulness of UTB disclosures. While some studies provide evidence that UTB disclosures reflect corporate tax shelter activities (e.g., Lisowsky et al., 2013, pp. 583–629), restrict earnings management (e.g., Gupta et al., 2016, pp. 1044–1074) and forecast future income tax cash outflows (e.g., Gleason et al., 2018, pp. 1–41), other studies document that UTB disclosures are often undervalued or overvalued (e.g., Dunbar et al., 2010, pp. 1–44), are influenced by management judgment (e.g., De Simone et al., 2014, pp. 456–472), do not reduce earnings management (e.g., Cazier et al., 2011, pp. 1–47), do not improve the ability to predict future income tax cash outflows (e.g., Robinson et al., 2016, pp. 1195–1217), increase audit costs (Erickson et al., 2016, pp. 67–85) and decrease investments in innovation (Goldman et al., 2020, pp. 1–52). Third, several recent papers consider UTBs disclosed under FIN 48 to be a suitable proxy for measuring corporate tax avoidance (e.g., Alexander et al., 2009, pp. 1–52; Lisowsky et al., 2013, pp. 583–629; De Simone et al., 2019, pp. 1536–1561). However, despite the advantages over all other tax avoidance measures, UTBs are not a clean measure of tax avoidance due to the contradicting research findings mentioned above (Hanlon and Heitzman, 2010, p. 143).

2.3 Accounting for Uncertain Tax Positions under IFRIC 23

2.3.1 Background

Accounting for uncertain tax positions in IFRS financial statements is regulated in IFRIC 23, an interpretation of IAS 12, Income Taxes (IASB, 2017, p. 5). The IFRS Interpretations Committee (IFRS IC) of the IASB issued IFRIC 23 on June 7, 2017 (IASB, 2017, p. 5; Schulz-Danso, 2020, rec. 17). On October 24, 2018, the interpretation was adopted by the European Union in its Official Journal and thus incorporated into binding European law (EU, 2018, pp. L 265/3 et seq.).

In the run-up to IFRIC 23, the IFRS IC already dealt with accounting for uncertain tax positions (Ruberg, 2016, p. 6). As part of the convergence project of the FASB and IASB, the regulations of IAS 12 should be revised and loopholes regarding the accounting for uncertain tax positions should be closed (IASB, 2002, p. 3). However, the proposals in the exposure draft ED/2009/2 led to an approval rate of less than 20 percent in the comment letters, so that the FASB and IASB decided not to finalize them (IASB, 2009, p. 1; Loitz, 2009, p. 2270). New incentives for addressing this issue were raised by the question submitted to the IFRS IC as to whether IAS 12, Income Taxes, and the probable threshold or IAS 37, Provisions, Contingent Liabilities and Contingent Assets, and the virtual certain threshold should be applied to the recognition of uncertain tax assets and liabilities (IASB, 2014a, rec. 6). With reference to IAS 12.12, the IFRS IC came to the conclusion that uncertain tax positions must be recognized if the payment or reimbursement is probable and published a corresponding agenda decision, known as NIFRIC, on July 15, 2014 (IASB, 2014a, rec. 6). Nevertheless, the IFRS IC observed diverse methods regarding various aspects of the recognition and measurement of uncertain tax positions (IASB, 2017, rec. BC2). IFRIC 23 aims to reduce this diversity and to improve the consistency and transparency of accounting for uncertain tax positions (IASB, 2017, p. 5; Loitz, 2017, p. M4).

2.3.2 Scope

All entities that prepare their financial statements in accordance with IFRS are obliged to apply IFRIC 23, as it is part of the IFRS Framework and has the same standing as an IFRS standard (IASB, 2017, rec. BC6). For European entities, the interpretation is to be applied indirectly through the endorsement process, while it can apply directly to non-European entities (EU, 2018, p. L 265/3).

IFRIC 23 is effective for all fiscal years beginning on or after January 1, 2019, whereby earlier application was permitted (IASB, 2017, rec. B1). Two transition methods were provided for initial application: the adjustments could be recorded in the year of implementation by recognizing the cumulative effect of the first-time application, or retrospectively by applying IAS 8 (IASB, 2017, rec. B2).

The material scope of the interpretation includes all tax treatments within the scope of IAS 12 (IASB, 2017, rec. 4). These comprise all domestic and foreign income taxes, including withholding taxes (Lüdenbach, Hoffmann and Freiberg, 2020, rec. 6). Other forms of taxes are subject to the rules in IAS 37 and IFRIC 21 (Schäuble, Lachmann, Bastini and Getzin, 2018, p. 433). IFRIC 23 applies to tax treatments that are used or intended to be used by an entity in its tax returns regarding both current and deferred taxes (IASB, 2017, rec. BC5).

The scope of IFRIC 23 is expanded by a reference in IFRS 3.24, Business Combinations, to the extent that deferred taxes arising from assets acquired and liabilities assumed are accounted for under IAS 12 and, if there is uncertainty, they fall under IFRIC 23 (IASB, 2017, rec. BC24). However, the treatment of current taxes acquired is not addressed (IASB, 2017, rec. BC23). Accounting for interest and penalties in connection with uncertain tax treatments is only subject to the interpretation as long as IAS 12 applies (IASB, 2017, rec. BC9).

2.3.3 Recognition

A key preliminary question for accounting for uncertain tax treatments is the definition of the adequate unit of account (Kämpfer, 2017, p. 455). This can be the entire tax calculation in a particular jurisdiction, each uncertain tax treatment separately, or a group of uncertain tax treatments (EY, 2017, p. 7). IFRIC 23 does not prescribe a specific unit of account to be used, but requires the management to make individual discretionary decisions based on the approach that better predicts the consequences of resolving the uncertainty (IASB, 2017, rec. 6). Thereby, influencing factors are the way in which the entity prepares its tax returns, as well as the way in which the tax authorities are expected to conduct their audit (IASB, 2017, rec. 6). In the case of different tax treatments, an individual consideration is appropriate (Dettmer and Heintges, 2016, p. 80). The tax deductibility of an expense item can be mentioned as an example (IASB, 2015, rec. IE2). However, in the case of similar tax treatments, a joint consideration is not necessarily appropriate (Kovermann and Velte, 2017, p. 406). If similar tax treatments are distributed among the responsibilities of different tax authorities in different jurisdictions and different tax assessments can be expected, a separate consideration would also be appropriate for similar tax treatments. As an example, the application of mutual agreements and arbitration procedures under the EU Arbitration Convention can be mentioned (IASB, 2015, rec. IE7). If, however, only one tax authority is responsible and a uniform assessment of similar tax treatments can be expected, the tax treatments should be included in a joint consideration (Dettmer and Heintges, 2016, p. 80). An example of this is transfer pricing risks (IASB, 2015, rec. IE3). However, it is no longer permitted to classify an entire tax return as a unit of account (Ruberg, 2017, p. 4).

In assessing uncertain tax treatments, entities must assume that the tax authorities will review all tax treatments they are entitled to examine and that they will have full knowledge of all information relevant for assessment (IASB, 2017, rec. 8). The term 'tax authority' also includes tax courts (IASB, 2017, rec. 3b). The detection risk is therefore not considered (Meyer, 2017, p. 1772).

An entity must assess whether it is probable that the tax authority, or in last instance the tax court, will accept an uncertain tax treatment or a group of uncertain tax treatments as reported in the tax return upon examination (IASB, 2017, rec. 9). The probable threshold is not defined in IFRIC 23. However, for issues within the scope of IAS 12, the probable threshold has to be equated with the more-likely-than-not threshold of 50 percent in analogy to the NIFRIC agenda decision in July 2014 (Gloth and Lüdders, 2017, p. 1858). If the recognition threshold is met, the entity must not reflect any uncertainty and recognizes the tax treatment in its financial statement consistently with the entire amount reported in its tax return (IASB, 2017, rec. 10). Thereby, all probabilities exceeding the probable threshold of 50 percent are treated the same way as a 100 percent probability (EY, 2017, p. 11). If, however, the recognition threshold is not met, the entity must reflect the effect of tax uncertainty in its financial statements (IASB, 2017, rec. 11). The amount is determined in the subsequent measurement step. Consistent judgments and estimates must be made for both current and deferred taxes (IASB, 2017, rec. 12).

2.3.4 Measurement

If a tax treatment does not meet the probable recognition threshold, it is necessary to measure the amount of tax uncertainty that needs to be taken into account in determining the taxable profit or loss, tax bases, unused tax losses and credits, and tax rates (IASB, 2017, rec. 11). The measurement should be carried out using either the most likely amount method or the expected value method, depending on which method better predicts the resolution of the uncertainty (IASB, 2017, rec. 11). Other measurement methods such as the cumulative probability approach are not permitted under IFRIC 23 (IASB, 2017, rec. BC18). In applying both methods, all possible outcomes of the tax uncertainties must first be estimated, and then the probability of occurring must be assigned to each outcome (IASB, 2017, rec. IE4). The most likely amount method chooses the outcome with the highest probability, while the expected value method determines the sum of the probability-weighted amounts of all possible outcomes (IASB, 2017, rec. IE5). The most likely amount method better predicts the resolution of uncertainty if the possible outcomes are binary or concentrate on one value (IASB, 2017, rec. 11a). This is the case, for example, with the question of whether or not a business expense is permitted as deductible (Kovermann and Velte, 2017, p. 407). The expected value method is preferable if the possible outcomes are spread over a wide range and are neither binary nor concentrate on one value (IASB, 2017, rec. 11b). This can be the case in the event of uncertainties with regard to transfer pricing (Jacob and Kazuch, 2018, p. 209). In analyzing uncertain tax treatments, all information available through the date of issuing the financial statements have to be considered (Penatzer, 2018, p. 779).

At the end of each reporting period, all tax treatments must be reassessed based on new facts and circumstances regarding their recognition and measurement (IASB, 2017, rec. 13). Examples for this are judgments by tax authorities on same or similar issues, changes in tax law or the expiry of the assessment period (IASB, 2017, rec. A2). The absence of an agreement or disagreement by a tax authority does not constitute new facts or information (IASB, 2017, rec. A3). In accordance with IAS 8, adjustments have to be recognized in profit or loss in the periods in which the new facts and circumstances arise, and for events after the balance sheet date, the regulations in IAS 10 apply (IASB, 2017, rec. 14).

2.3.5 Presentation and Disclosure

If it is probable that the tax authority will not accept a tax treatment, the determined amount of tax uncertainty will differ from the amount reported in the tax return. Therefore, the amount measured needs to be taken into account in determining the taxable profit or loss, tax bases, unused tax losses, unused tax credits, and tax rates (IASB, 2017, rec. 11). The current taxes payable have to be classified as current, provided that income taxes are paid within 12 months, while deferred taxes always have to be classified as non-current (Penatzer, 2018, p. 779).

IFRIC 23 does not expand the disclosure requirements, but refers to the existing general disclosure requirements in IAS 1 regarding tax-related contingencies as well as significant judgements, assumptions and estimates made in determining current and deferred taxes (IASB, 2017, rec. A4 et seq.; EY, 2017, p. 18).

Appendix C summarizes the accounting regulations according to IFRIC 23 and the individual steps for their implementation.

2.3.6 Empirical Insights

To date, no empirical studies have been conducted on IFRIC 23. As part of the FIN 48 research, a few studies compare income tax reporting between US GAAP and IFRS (e.g., Atwood et al., 2012, pp. 1–44; Gleason et al., 2018, pp. 1–41; Lee and Swenson, 2010, pp. 222–233). However, these studies were conducted before IFRIC 23 was issued, so that their comparison is no longer tenable. Although the two interpretations are conceptually similar, there are significant differences, as outlined in Chapter 3, that require additional research on IFRIC 23. Future work should examine the implications of adopting IFRIC 23, including changes in information quality, comparability, costs and usage. Changes in information quality occur if the quantity, quality or relevance of the reported information change. Information comparability can be examined by comparing the information disclosed before and after the adoption and by comparing accounting for uncertain tax positions under IFRS, US GAAP and local GAAP. Information costs include implementation, audit and capital costs. Lastly, information usage relates to how the new information is used by management for tax avoidance, earnings management, management compensation and investment decision-making, as well as by auditors, analysts, investors and researchers.

3 Critical Analysis of the Conceptual Differences between FIN 48 and IFRIC 23

3.1 Background

At first glance, the rules for accounting for uncertain tax positions under US GAAP and IFRS appear to be generally similar in their approach. Both FIN 48 and IFRIC 23 are an interpretation of the respective accounting standard for income taxes, result from diverse accounting practices, and their overall objective is to provide uniform accounting guidelines with respect to uncertain tax positions (FASB, 2006, rec. 2; IASB, 2017, rec. BC2). A detailed analysis, however, reveals distinct differences between the two interpretations which can lead to different accounting results when considering uncertainty in income taxes. The fact that there are differences is already apparent prior to analysis, given that IFRIC 23 only contains 12 recitals and 19 pages, while FIN 48 contains 24 recitals and 47 pages, and thus provides far less details (Loitz, 2017, p. M5). Hereafter, the most important differences are discussed and assessed critically.

3.2 Scope

First of all, FIN 48 and IFRIC 23 use different terminologies for uncertain tax positions but define them similarly. FIN 48 refers to the term 'uncertain tax position' (FASB, 2006, rec. 4), while IFRIC 23 uses the term 'uncertain tax treatment' (IASB, 2017, rec. 3). Since the rules in IFRIC 23 are basically guided by the long-standing FIN 48, the IASB must have deliberately decided not to

Supplementary Information The online version contains supplementary material available at https://doi.org/10.1007/978-3-658-39041-9_3.

C. Seibert, *Differences between FIN 48 and IFRIC 23*, BestMasters,
https://doi.org/10.1007/978-3-658-39041-9_3

adapt the same wording. On the one hand, the different terminologies simplify the distinction between the accounting principles. On the other hand, using the same wording would remove any confusion or misunderstanding and contribute to greater convergence between the accounting standards. However, this difference is rather of formal nature and does not have any significant practical accounting implications, as the same issues are subsumed under both terms (FASB, 2006, rec. 4; IASB, 2017, rec. 3).

The personal scope does not differ between the interpretations. Both FIN 48 and IFRIC 23 are applicable to all entities that prepare their financial statements in accordance with US GAAP, respectively, IFRS (FASB, 2006, rec. 1; IASB 2017, rec. 1). However, this has different repercussions. FIN 48 applies to US entities, foreign subsidiaries of US entities, US subsidiaries of foreign entities, and foreign entities registered with the SEC (Treasure, 2007, p. 2). Therefore, FIN 48 is also binding for German companies with a US parent company or with subsidiaries in the USA (Schön, 2007, p. 485). In contrast, IFRIC 23 is mandatory for entities in 166 jurisdictions (IFRS Foundation, 2020, p. 1). German listed companies have to follow IFRIC 23 as adopted by the EU (EU, 2018, p. L 265/3). The SEC, however, prohibits the application of IFRS and thus IFRIC 23 for US listed companies, but allows foreign SEC registrants to apply IFRS and IFRIC 23 (SEC, 2007, p. 1). Consequently, the two interpretations do not necessarily affect the same entities. However, for companies that prepare their financial statements in accordance with both IFRS and US GAAP, it is even more important to understand the differences between the two interpretations.

With regard to the temporal scope, the difference between the two interpretations is that FIN 48 only allows one transition method, namely the modified retrospective approach that recognizes the cumulative effect of initially applying the interpretation (FASB, 2006, rec. B72), while IFRIC 23 offers two methods to choose from, namely the full retrospective approach in accordance with IAS 8 and alternatively the modified retrospective approach that corresponds to the transition method under FIN 48 (IASB, 2017, rec. B2). However, the full retrospective approach under IFRIC 23 must be viewed critically. In practice, it is often very difficult to apply the full retrospective approach without incorporating hindsight due to the judgmental nature of accounting for uncertain tax positions (Grant Thornton, 2016, p. 5). In most cases, entities need to use a high level of hindsight to get all of the information they need to reconsider judgments in previous years (EY, 2005, pp. 15 et seq.). It is therefore helpful and appropriate to provide the modified transaction method as an alternative. Since this method is also provided under FIN 48, the provision of the alternative method increases the convergence between the two standards. However, it should be noted that a retrospective application is time-consuming and incurs additional costs for the preparation of information (Siemens, 2016, p. 4). In addition, a change in the amount of uncertain tax positions implies a change in the estimate which would normally be accounted for prospectively in accordance with IAS 8 (BDO, 2016, pp. 5 et seq.). For these reasons, it makes sense to apply FIN 48 and IFRIC 23 prospectively on initial adoption (Nestle, 2016, p. 3).

The material scope of the interpretations differs in several points. The only commonality between FIN 48 and IFRIC 23 in this regard is that they apply to all tax positions within the scope of their respective accounting standards (FASB, 2006, rec. 3; IASB, 2017, rec. 4). Since FIN 48 and IFRIC 23 are the interpretations of FAS 109 and IAS 12, it is appropriate that their scope relates to income taxes only (BDO, 2005, p. 2; DRSC, 2016, p. 2). However, uncertain tax positions can also arise in the context of other, non-income-based taxes. In this case, the provisions of FAS 5 and IAS 37 apply (Deloitte, 2007, p. 4; Schäuble et al., 2018, p. 433). Uncertain tax positions related to other taxes are often subject to the same examination procedures by the same tax authorities as uncertain tax positions related to income taxes (Mazars, 2016, p. 4). Nevertheless, this similarity is not reflected in the accounting rules. Instead, FAS 5 and IAS 37 require different recognition thresholds and measurement methods compared to FIN 48 and IFRIC 23 (Nestle, 2016, p. 2). FAS 5 uses a probable recognition threshold and the best estimate method for measurement, and IAS 37 uses the virtually certain recognition threshold and the expected value method (EY, 2005, p. 4; EY, 2016, p. 3). This inconsistency between the accounting for uncertain tax positions related to income taxes and the accounting for uncertain tax positions related to other taxes is not covered by FIN 48 and IFRIC 23. Standard setters should address this issue in future (DRSC, 2016, p. 2), as it is of particular relevance when uncertainties between income taxes and other taxes are interrelated, for example, when the uncertainty over the treatment of a particular tax affects the amount that is deductible for income tax purposes (Mazars, 2016, p. 4).

Income tax uncertainties associated with assets acquired and liabilities assumed in a business combination are captured by the material scope of both FIN 48 and IFRIC 23. However, while the recognition and measurement criteria in FIN 48 apply to both current and deferred taxes (FASB, 2006, rec. C4), those under IFRIC 23 apply to deferred taxes only (IASB, 2017, rec. BC23). A uniform treatment of current and deferred taxes as under FIN 48 is to be advocated, as this simplifies acquisition accounting and accounting for uncertain tax positions (TEI, 2005, p. 13). Even after the acquiring entity has reviewed the acquired entity's tax returns and related documents, it is often difficult in practice to determine the appropriate current and deferred taxes to be recognized (BB&T, 2005, p. 3). Different recognition and measurement principles for current and deferred taxes further complicate the determination of the amounts to be recognized (KPMG, 2016, p. 7). In addition, under IFRS, distortions can occur if current taxes are accounted for in accordance with IFRS 3, while deferred taxes are accounted for according to IAS 12 and IFRIC 23 (IASB, 2017, rec. BC24). In applying IFRS 3, entities can take the detection risk into account when measuring current taxes at fair value (EY, 2016, p. 5). In contrast, IFRIC 23 requires that entities do not consider a detection risk (IASB, 2017, rec. 8). Thus, measurement inconsistencies arise. Therefore, the rules in paragraph IN 9 of IFRS 3, which state that both current and deferred taxes are within the scope of IAS 12, should prevail, and not the rules in paragraph 24 of IFRS 3, which only refer to deferred taxes (Mazars, 2016, p. 4). Accordingly, a revision of the requirements in paragraph 24 of IFRS 3 may be advisable (EFRAG, 2016, p. 2).

Accounting for interest and penalties associated with uncertain tax positions create additional differences between US GAAP and IFRS. Under US GAAP, they are accounted for under FIN 48 (FASB, 2006, rec. 15), while under IFRS, they are only covered by the scope of IAS 12 and IFRIC 23 if interest and penalties meet the definition of income taxes; otherwise, they are accounted for under IAS 37 (IASB, 2017, rec. BC9). It is more appropriate if only one accounting standard applies to the accounting for interest and penalties (Deloitte, 2005, p. 9). FIN 48 applies the recognition and measurement requirements of uncertain tax positions consistently to interest and penalties (KPMG, 2005, p. 4). Due to the interactions between uncertain tax positions and interest and penalties, this is to be welcomed. The interactive nature makes it difficult to distinguish between uncertain tax positions and interest and penalties (Deloitte, 2016, p. 3). However, under IFRS, a clear distinction is needed in order to assess whether interest and penalties fall within the scope of IFRIC 23 (IASB, 2017, rec. BC9). As a result, different recognition thresholds and measurement principles can apply to similar items. For example, PwC, KPMG and Deloitte allow an accounting policy choice between IAS 12 and IAS 37, while EY prefers IAS 37 (KPMG, 2016, p. 3). This favors the emergence of diverse practices, while the purpose of the interpretation is to restrict diversity in practice (IASB, 2017, p. 5). If interest and penalties are fully covered by the scope of IAS 12 and IFRIC 23, diversity in practice would further be reduced, which is the intent of the interpretation.

3.3 Recognition

Prior to the recognition and measurement of uncertain tax positions, under both FIN 48 and IFRIC 23, the unit of account must be determined (FASB, 2006, rec. 5; IASB, 2017, rec. 6). The levels at which uncertain tax positions can be aggregated and the decision bases for determining the unit of account are similar under both interpretations (Deloitte, 2007, p. 11; EY, 2017, p. 7). However, there are minor differences in the wording of these requirements which can lead to the same issues being treated differently (KPMG, 2017, p. 6). For example, an uncertain tax position can be considered separately from other positions according to FIN 48, while it would be considered together with those under IFRIC 23, and vice versa (KPMG, 2018, p. 8). The determination of the unit of account is at the discretion of the entities and depends on whether the entity will follow the entity-specific approach, which is based on how entities prepare their tax return, or the tax authority's approach, which is based on how they carry out their audit (FASB, 2006, rec. 5; IASB, 2017, rec. 6). Problems can arise under FIN 48 if the two approaches are in conflict, for example, if according to the entity-specific approach an individual consideration of uncertain tax positions is appropriate, while the tax authority's approach concludes that a collective consideration is appropriate. In this case, entities have a decision problem and choose the level of aggregation that is more favorable to them (TEI, 2005, p. 19). Typically, higher levels of aggregation are preferred in order to reach the recognition threshold and to avoid the high burden of documenting at lower levels (AcSEC, 2005, p. 5). This problem is resolved in IFRIC 23 by stipulating that in such cases the approach that better predicts the resolution of the uncertainty should be followed, which will usually be the approach of the tax authorities (Deloitte, 2016, p. 4). This additional provision restricts the entities' arbitrary scope for action and results in a higher degree of consistency in the financial statements.

Both FIN 48 and IFRIC 23 stipulate that the detection risk is not to be considered in analyzing uncertain tax positions (FASB, 2006, rec. B14; IASB, 2017, rec. 8). Even if the two interpretations have the greatest commonality in this aspect, there might be differences with regard to the tax authorities' right to examine income tax returns. What the tax authorities are allowed to investigate depends on the statutory provisions of the respective country (Kämpfer, 2017, p. 457). In Germany, a tax audit is no longer permitted if the period for assessment has expired as per Sec. 169 Para. 1 AO, or if the review is repealed as per Sec. 164 Para. 3 AO (Meyer, 2015, p. 2926). In other countries, however, the right of the tax authorities to carry out tax audits might not be limited in time so that they can examine uncertain tax positions at any time in the future (Business

Europe, 2016, p. 4). In these cases, an exception to the existing regulation could be useful that allows the probability of detection to be taken into account (Grove Tax Policy Institute, 2016, pp. 3 et seq.). This would also be in line with the long-standing jurisdiction of the German Federal Fiscal Court dated October 19, 1993 that a provision for tax audit risks can only be recognized if the relevant issue has already been taken up by the tax authority or if this is at least imminent (BFH, 1993, p. 891). However, this view is increasingly controversial in the German commercial law literature due to the creditor protection function and the principle of prudence (Herzig and Liekenbrock, 2013, p. 410).

From a conceptual point of view, FIN 48 and IFRIC 23 do not differ in terms of their approach and calculation method. Both interpretations implemented a two-step approach consisting of a recognition and a subsequent measurement step (FASB, 2006, rec. B27; IASB, 2017, rec. 9–11). Therefore, two separate analyses must be performed and the uncertainty associated with a tax position is addressed through both the recognition threshold and the measurement approach (KPMG, 2005, p. 2). In addition, both regulations recognize uncertain tax positions using a benefit recognition approach (FASB, 2006, rec. B15 et seq.; Deloitte, 2018, p. 2). This approach only recognizes an asset if the respective recognition criteria are met (IASB/FASB, 2005, rec. 15). Through the recognition of a tax benefit, the tax liability is then implicitly reduced. Before IFRIC 23 was introduced, the liability recognition approach was applied under IFRS (Kessler and Scholz-Görlach, 2009, p. 289). In contrast to the benefit recognition approach, the liability recognition approach always recognizes a tax benefit (IASB/FASB, 2005, rec. 15). A corresponding tax liability is then recorded as a compensation. This conceptual change under IFRS regarding an alignment to the US GAAP approach is to be welcomed, as it increases the convergence between the two accounting regulations. However, the choice of the recognition approach is more of a technical question with no practical accounting implications. In the end, both approaches lead to the same balance sheet result, unless different recognition and measurement criteria are stipulated (IASB/FASB, 2005, rec. 16).

Although FIN 48 and IFRIC 23 apply the same recognition approach, their approaches differ in content and structure. First, the two interpretations established different recognition criteria. In order to assess whether an uncertain tax position should be recognized, US GAAP accountants must ask themselves whether it is more likely than not that the tax position reported will be sustained upon examination (FASB, 2006, rec. 6). IFRS accountants, however, ask themselves whether it is probable that the tax treatment reported will be accepted upon examination (IASB, 2017, rec. 9). Accordingly, under FIN 48, the more-likely-than-not threshold must be reached, which is explicitly defined as a likelihood of more than 50 percent (FASB, 2006, rec. 6). IFRIC 23 applies the probable threshold but does not define what can be considered as probable (Kovermann and Velte, 2017, p. 408). Thus, FIN 48 is formulated much more precisely. The meaning of the term 'probable' differs between entities and between accounting standards. In the US GAAP accounting practice, 'probable' is interpreted as a threshold of 70 to 80 percent (Morgan Stanley, 2005, p. 2), while in the IFRS accounting practice, it is generally defined as 'more likely than not', i.e., a probability greater than 50 percent (EY, 2016, p. 5). In order to ensure a consistent application, the IASB should clarify that 'probable' should be defined as 'more likely than not' (EFRAG, 2016, p. 3). Even if the same level of probability is applied under FIN 48 and IFRIC 23, their terminologies still differ. The term 'more likely than not' should be used under both interpretations as it is better understood and applied more easily in practice (Morgan Stanley, 2005, p. 2). Nonetheless, it is legitimate that IFRIC 23 uses the term 'probable' as this wording is consistent with IAS 12 and other aspects of the IFRS accounting framework (PwC, 2016, p. 2). Since the use of different formulations has no direct accounting impact, applying the same level of probability is sufficient to ensure consistency and comparability in accounting for uncertain tax positions.

Second, a comparison of the interpretations reveals an inverse question structure. FIN 48 first assumes that there is no tax benefit recognized and then examines whether some level of the tax position will be sustained upon examination (FASB, 2006, rec. 6; KPMG, 2018, p. 9). IFRIC 23, on the other hand, assumes that the full amount has to be recognized and examines afterwards whether the tax position will be accepted by the tax authority (IASB, 2017, rec. 9; KPMG, 2018, p. 9). Consequently, an uncertain tax position is recognized under FIN 48 if the recognition question is answered in the affirmative and the recognition threshold is reached (FASB, 2006, rec. 8), while under IFRIC 23, an uncertain tax position is recognized if the question is answered in the negative and the threshold is not reached (IASB, 2017, rec. 11). In other words, according to FIN 48, uncertain tax positions are recorded if the result of the assessment is in the favor of the taxable entity (FASB, 2006, rec. 6), while according to IFRIC 23, they are recognized if the result is in the favor of the tax authority (Penatzer, 2018, p. 780). There is no objective better or worse with regard to the question structure as both are justifiable depending on the argumentation and point of view. However, the question structure under IFRIC 23 seems to be more intuitive and therefore more appropriate since entities do not have to make complex and uncertain estimates of outcomes in a subsequent measurement step if a rejection by the tax authority is unlikely (Grant Thornton, 2016, p. 3).

Third, the recognition scenarios differ between FIN 48 and IFRIC 23. While FIN 48 distinguishes between different levels of tax benefits that are sustained upon examination (Kimmelfield et al., 2006, p. 294), IFRIC 23 only takes into account the full acceptance of tax treatments without the possibility of partial acceptance or rejection (Grant Thornton, 2016, p. 3). Regardless of whether there is a 60 or 100 percent probability that a particular tax deduction will be accepted by the tax authority, entities account for 100 percent of the tax deduction under IFRIC 23 (EY, 2017, p. 11). Under FIN 48, entities only account for 100 percent if the tax deduction will be sustained with a 100 percent probability (FASB, 2006, rec. A19 et seq.). With a probability of 60 percent, the amount recognized is determined in the subsequent measurement step (FASB, 2006, rec. 8). In the event that the recognition threshold is not reached, for example with a probability of 40 percent, entities do not recognize a tax benefit under FIN 48 and apply the measurement step under IFRIC 23 (FASB, 2006, rec. 8; IASB, 2017, rec. 11). If no distinction is made between a likelihood of 51 and 100 percent, the probability assessment and determination of the unit of account are highly sensitive to manipulation since these aspects decide over reaching the recognition threshold and the accounting consequences (EY, 2016, p. 5). Therefore, considering different scenarios of acceptance as under FIN 48 is more appropriate.

Fourth and lastly, US GAAP accountants only take into account the technical merits of a tax position when assessing the recognition threshold, e.g., negotiations with tax authorities are not considered (FASB, 2006, rec. 6). IFRS accountants, however, also consider the possibility of settlement which is to be welcomed (IASB, 2017, rec. 13). Entities operating in jurisdictions with less developed legal and tax systems are often unable to reliably assess the recognition threshold based solely on the technical merits and achieve an all-or-nothing outcome (PwC, 2005, p. 5; Morgan Stanley, 2005, p. 3). Therefore, it is more operational that the assessment is based on all available evidence including the outcome of potential settlement negotiations.

3.4 Measurement

To determine the value of uncertainty, different measurement methods are used under FIN 48 and IFRIC 23. According to FIN 48, the valuation has to be carried out using the cumulative probability method (FASB, 2006, rec. 8). IFRIC 23, in contrast, stipulates the use of the most likely amount method or the expected value method, depending on which method better predicts the resolution of the uncertainty (IASB, 2017, rec. 11). The cumulative probability method prescribed by FIN 48 is explicitly prohibited under IFRIC 23 (IASB, 2017, rec. BC18). All three measurement methods require to estimate the possible outcomes of the tax uncertainty, to assign the probability of occurring to each outcome and to sort the outcomes in descending order according to the amount (FASB, 2006, rec. A21; IASB, 2017, rec. IE4). However, the application of these methods to the same situation can lead to different amounts being recorded (IASB, 2014b, rec. A1). An exemplary computational comparison of the three measurement methods can be found in Appendix D.

Table 2 in Appendix D relates to the case where the range of potential additional tax payments is large. In this example, US GAAP accountants recognize a tax benefit of CU 600,000, while IFRS accountants record an uncertain tax position of CU 470,000 using the expected value method or CU 800,000 using the most likely amount method. Since the expected value method better predicts the resolution of the uncertainty, this method is used pursuant to IFRIC 23. Consequently, the liability accounted for under FIN 48 is significantly higher than the liability accounted for under IFRIC 23. In other situations, the amount calculated in accordance with IFRIC 23 may also exceed the amount calculated under FIN 48 (KPMG, 2005, p. 5). This example gives clear evidence that the valuation of uncertain tax positions can vary significantly depending on the measurement method. As a result, US GAAP and IFRS financial statements are not comparable. Since the determined amounts of tax liabilities also form the basis for calculating interest and penalties, these can differ in terms of the amount as well (AICPA, 2006, p. 6). In addition, the different approaches can also affect the accounting for deferred taxes, as it is often not a question of whether deductions are accepted by the tax authorities, but over what period of time they will be asserted (FASB, 2007, rec. A27). Therefore, the amount of deferred tax assets on loss carryforwards can be impaired as well (FASB, 2007, rec. 17).

Table 3 in Appendix D provides an example where only two outcomes are likely to occur. While under US GAAP, a tax benefit of CU 200,000 is recognized, under IFRS, the uncertain tax position is recognized with an amount of CU 140,000 using the expected value method or an amount of CU 200,000 using the most likely amount method, whereby the latter has to be applied because the most likely amount method better predicts the resolution of the uncertainty. Consequently, FIN 48 and IFRIC 23 lead to the same result in this example, and the financial statements according to US GAAP and IFRS are comparable.

According to the FASB, the cumulative probability approach ensures a true and fair view of the financial statements, as it leads to a consistent and comparable valuation of uncertain tax positions (FASB, 2006, rec. B44). The asset, financial and earnings position is presented more accurately compared to the most likely amount method but less faithfully compared to the expected value method (FASB, 2006, rec. B44). The cumulative probability method can be viewed as a mixture of the expected value approach and the most likely amount approach. It considers outcomes with low probabilities, but does not include all possible outcomes in its calculation (FASB, 2006, rec. A22). Since the largest amount of the tax benefit that has a cumulative probability of occurring greater than 50 percent is recognized, the cumulative probability approach contains an implicit recognition threshold of 50 percent (IASB, 2011, rec. 30). Therefore, this method is best suited if outliers are not important or subject to a greater estimation uncertainty than central outcomes (IASB, 2011, rec. 35). In addition, the cumulative probability method is easier to measure but not necessarily less useful than the expected value approach. If the benefits of the expected value approach do not outweigh their higher costs, the cumulative probability method could be used as a viable alternative (IASB, 2011, rec. 36). The IASB, however, expressed clear opposition to this method, as the possibility of additionally using the cumulative probability method would make it even more difficult for companies to judge which method better predicts the resolution of the uncertainty (IASB, 2017, rec. BC18). Moreover, the IASB does not permit the application of this method, as it is not used in any of the other IFRS standards (IASB, 2017, rec. BC18).

The expected value approach is conceptually of very high quality. It corresponds to the true and fair view approach (FASB, 2006, rec. B44) and works particularly well with a large number of possible outcomes (IASB, 2017, rec. 4). Compared to the other measurement methods, it takes into account all possible outcomes, including those with very low probabilities (FASB, 2006, rec. B26). Thus, the assessed situations contain more information, and as a result, the expected value approach contributes to an improved quality of financial statements (IASB/FASB, 2005, rec. 33). Both the taxpayer and the tax authorities tend to adopt the expected value approach when it comes to reaching agreements in disputes that are acceptable to both parties (Harvey, 2005, p. 5). In a tax audit, often neither the taxpayer's nor the tax authority's position is fully complied with (EY, 2005, p. 10). Rather, the actual result lies somewhere between the two viewpoints, just like the expected value. With regard to the accounting effects, the expected value approach is therefore very close to the actual result after the disputed matters have been settled (Penatzer, 2018, p. 780). However, the advantages have to be set against a few disadvantages. The expected value approach is associated with a high level of effort and complexity, as it requires the establishment of several scenarios with the corresponding probabilities of occurrence (IASB, 2017, rec. IE4). In the course of this, the first difficulty is to identify all individual outcomes, where the number of all outcomes is unknown, and the second difficulty is to assign an individual probability to each outcome (ACCA, 2016, p. 5). Thereby, a level of precision is required that is rarely found in the settlement of disputes (TEI, 2005, p. 16). The evaluation of settlement probabilities is rather speculative in nature (EY, 2005, p. 10). This gives rise to the danger that the estimated probabilities are selected in such a way that the desired amount of tax liability is recognized (Penatzer, 2018, p. 780). In addition, the expected value approach is sensitive to extreme and relatively unlikely outcomes (IASB, 2011, rec. 18). Moreover, although the expected value method contains components of a fair value assessment, at the same time, it violates its essential premises, since it excludes present value concepts and risk premiums (EY, 2005, p. 10). This was the decisive reason for the FASB not to allow this measurement method (FASB, 2006, rec. B26).

The most likely amount approach is simple to understand and easy to measure (IASB/FASB, 2005, rec. 32). Moreover, it works particularly well if the possible outcomes are binary (IASB, 2017, rec. 4). As it only has to be decided whether or not the 50 percent threshold will be exceeded, this method includes an implicit recognition threshold such as the cumulative probability approach (IASB, 2011, rec. 43). The most likely amount method is less cumbersome and time-consuming than the cumulative probability approach and the expected value approach because several different outcomes do not have to be assessed if a high individual probability of occurrence is expected for one outcome (Kämpfer, 2017, p. 458). In addition, the most likely amount method is not sensitive to outliers (IASB, 2011, rec. 43). Consequently, this measurement method can be used as a suitable alternative if the benefits of the other methods do not outweigh their higher costs (IASB, 2011, rec. 46). The downside of the most likely amount method is, however, that it will lead to wrong results when there are more than two possible outcomes and peaks (IASB, 2011, rec. 45). Moreover, potential values can be systematically neglected which in turn leads to a low information content (IASB/FASB, 2005, rec. 33). In addition, there is the risk that the most likely amount is only roughly estimated so that the result obtained is not trustworthy and financial statements may become misleading (PwC, 2005, p. 7).

When measuring the amount of uncertainty, both interpretations take into account the outcome of negotiations between the taxpayer and tax authority (FASB, 2006, rec. 8; IASB, 2017, rec. 13). This equivalence between the interpretations is to be welcomed. However, compared to the recognition step, there is an inconsistency under FIN 48 and a consistency under IFRIC 23 (FASB, 2006, rec. 6; IASB, 2017, rec. 13). As explained in Section 3.3, it is therefore advisable to align FIN 48 with IFRIC 23.

At the end of each reporting period, both FIN 48 and IFRIC 23 require entities to review whether the recognition and measurement of uncertain tax positions need to be reassessed due to changed facts and circumstances or new information (FASB, 2006, rec. 12; IASB, 2017, rec. 13). This is to be welcomed as reevaluations are crucial to adequately reflect the impact of uncertainty on income taxes (ACCA, 2016, p. 4). However, FIN 48 only takes into account information available at the reporting date (FASB, 2006, rec. B38). New findings that arise in the period between the reporting date and the time of preparation are not considered in the recognition and measurement analyses (FASB, 2006, rec. B47). Thus, changes after the reporting date are always treated as non-adjusting events (DRSC, 2016, pp. 4 et seq.). If subsequent events have a significant impact on the recognition or measurement of uncertain tax positions, entities are required to disclose them in the notes to the financial statements (FASB, 2006, rec. 21). This is an exception to the general guidance on subsequent events under FASB Statement No. 165, which is now regulated under ASC 855 (KPMG, 2017, p. 9). IFRIC 23, on the other hand, takes into account all information available through the date the financial statements are issued (IASB, 2017, rec. 13). Thereby, changes in facts and circumstances occurring after the reporting date are assessed in accordance with IAS 10 in order to determine whether they are treated as adjusting or non-adjusting events (IASB, 2017, rec. 14). Thus, this regulation is in line with the general guidance in IAS 10 (Telefonica, 2016, p. 4). To ensure a consistent accounting for subsequent changes, the rules set out in IFRIC 23 are more appropriate than the rules stipulated under FIN 48.

3.5 Presentation and Disclosure

As a result of the application of FIN 48 and IFRIC 23, there is a difference between the amount declared in the tax return and the amount of uncertainty measured based on the interpretations (FASB, 2006, rec. 17, IASB, 2017, rec. 10 et seq.). This circumstance is taken into account differently by the two interpretations. Under FIN 48, an income tax liability must be recognized at the differential amount, as this represents an unrecognized tax benefit (FASB, 2006, rec. 17), whereas under IFRIC 23, an income tax liability at the amount of tax uncertainty measured must be recorded (IASB, 2017, rec. 11). This difference in the amount of the tax liability to be recognized results conclusively from the differences in the recognition regulations presented in Section 3.3. Since FIN 48 first assumes that no tax benefit has to be recognized and then examines whether some level of the tax position will be sustained (FASB, 2006, rec. 6; KPMG, 2018, p. 9), it is adequate that the amount of the unrecognized tax benefit, which is the differential amount, has to be recorded. Furthermore, since IFRIC 23 first assumes that the full amount has to be recognized and then examines whether the tax treatment will be accepted (IASB, 2017, rec. 9; KPMG, 2018, p. 9), it is appropriate that the amount of the tax uncertainty measured is recognized. In addition, the amounts recognized can differ in their value due to the different measurement methods used as described in Section 3.4 (IASB, 2014b, rec. A1).

Moreover, the two interpretations provide different balance sheet classification criteria for income taxes payable. FIN 48 contains guidelines for the classification of the recognized amounts itself and states that the distinction between current and non-current liabilities depends on the timing of the expected cash payment (FASB, 2006, rec. 17). IFRIC 23 does not provide guidance on the balance sheet classification, but refers to the general classification requirements in IAS 1, according to which the classification depends on the existence of an unconditional right to postpone payment for at least twelve months after the reporting date (IASB, 2017, rec. A4). However, the different classification criteria do not lead to major differences in the financial statement presentation. Since in practice the time of preparing the tax return and the time of the final resolution of uncertain tax positions with the tax authorities are several years apart, uncertain tax liabilities are usually classified as non-current under both accounting regulations (FASB, 2006, rec. B56). Moreover, both FIN 48 and IFRIC 23 stipulate that uncertainties in income taxes are considered as part of the income tax accounts and not reported separately under provisions or other liabilities (FASB, 2006, rec. 17; IASB, 2019, p. 1). This leads to a higher level of consistency in financial reporting. Another common aspect of both accounting regulations is that deferred taxes must always be classified as non-current (FASB, 2006, rec. 18; IASB, 2017, rec. A4). Overall, these presentation and classification requirements enable a better comparability of US GAAP and IFRS financial statements.

With regard to the disclosure requirements, FIN 48 and IFRIC 23 differ from one another as well. In addition to the general disclosures in FASB Statement No. 5, FIN 48 introduces additional disclosure requirements on unrecognized tax benefits (FASB, 2006, rec. 21). IFRIC 23, however, does not contain new disclosure requirements but refers to the existing ones in IAS 1 and IAS 12 (IASB, 2017, rec. BC22). A comparison reveals that the disclosure requirements under FIN 48 are much more detailed than those under IFRIC 23. The comprehensive disclosure provisions of FIN 48 result in a more transparent reporting of the impact of uncertainties in income taxes and provide financial statement users with an adequate basis to identify the tax uncertainties and to evaluate managements' judgments (PwC, 2005, p. 10). Referring to FASB Statement No. 5 solely would result in the disclosure of very limited information on the effect of uncertainties on income tax positions (KPMG, 2005, pp. 4 et seq.). However, the extensive information disclosed will also be used by tax authorities in the context of tax audits which could adversely affect entities (FEI, 2005, p. 13). For example, it could limit their ability to defend their uncertain tax positions and their ability to negotiate a settlement (Hennig et al., 2008, p. 26). The reduction of reporting requirements under IFRIC 23 compared to FIN 48 is to be welcomed with regard to several aspects. From an economic point of view, the reduction is associated with less effort for preparers of financial statements (Grant Thornton, 2016, p. 4). Furthermore, from a practical point of view, no additional disclosures are required as the existing provisions present preparers sufficient guidance and provide financial statement users with relevant information (ESMA, 2016, p. 4). In addition, there is no need to question the added value of information about unrecognized tax benefits, and there is no risk of providing a roadmap to tax authorities for tax audits (Penatzer, 2018, p. 781).

3.6 Interim Conclusion

The comparison of the regulations for accounting for uncertain tax positions under US GAAP and IFRS shows that, despite some similarities between FIN 48 and IFRIC 23, there are several more or less significant differences between the interpretations that lead to different results when accounting for uncertain tax positions. Both FIN 48 and IFRIC 23 have reduced the heterogeneity within US GAAP and IFRS financial statements regarding the accounting for uncertain tax positions, but at the same time the heterogeneity between the two international accounting regulations has increased. The similarities and differences between FIN 48 and IFRIC 23 are summarized in tabular form in Appendix E.

4 Critical Analysis of the Practical Application of IFRIC 23

4.1 Perspective of Tax Authority

4.1.1 Analysis of the Results of the 2019 Tax Audit

Disagreements between taxpayers and tax authorities with regard to the tax treatment of business transactions are not uncommon. According to the German tax administration, 3,454,532 appeals and 64,925 lawsuits were filed with German tax authorities in the 2019 calendar year (BMF, 2020a, pp. 1 et seq.). This is mainly caused by tax audits as they often result in high additional tax payments to tax authorities. As reported by the German Federal Ministry of Finance, 13,341 tax auditors were deployed nationwide during the 2019 tax audit who audited a total of 181,345 companies and generated an additional result of 15.2 billion euros for the tax authorities (BMF, 2020b, p. 34). Thereof, 11.6 billion euros were gained by auditing large companies (BMF, 2020b, p. 36). Small companies had to make additional tax payments of 1.1 billion euros (BMF, 2020b, p. 36). The additional result that was achieved by tax authorities through interest in accordance with Sec. 233a AO amounted to 2.5 billion euros, which corresponds to around 16.7 percent of the total additional result (BMF, 2020b, p. 37).

An empirical study on the practice of tax audits in Germany published by PwC in 2019 provides information on the most frequent and largest tax audit findings (PwC, 2019, p. 1). In the area of income taxes, accruals are the most frequent audit area and their adjustments result in the largest tax back payments (PwC, 2019, p. 11). In addition, the tax treatment of restructuring operations,

---

Supplementary Information The online version contains supplementary material available at https://doi.org/10.1007/978-3-658-39041-9_4.

C. Seibert, *Differences between FIN 48 and IFRIC 23*, BestMasters,
https://doi.org/10.1007/978-3-658-39041-9_4

despite usually careful and intensive management, often raises objections (PwC, 2019, p. 17). Furthermore, fiscal entities for income tax purposes create significant additional tax burdens for companies (PwC, 2019, p. 17). In the area of international tax law, transfer pricing issues are a key audit area and regularly lead to substantial additional tax payments to the tax authorities (PwC, 2019, p. 18).

Publicly traded German companies must account for tax risks resulting from tax audits in accordance with the new IFRIC 23 requirements from January 1, 2019. Against this background, an expert interview on the challenges associated with IFRIC 23 was conducted with a tax auditor from the German tax authority for large and group audits. The interview guide is attached in Appendix F. The key findings of the interview are presented in the following two sections.

4.1.2 Challenges

With regard to the examination of tax treatments by tax authorities, companies must assume a detection risk of 100 percent, implying that the tax authorities will examine every tax position and have all the relevant information for their assessment (IASB, 2017, rec. 8). This has led to a shift in the methodology used by companies. While previously the crucial question was whether a controversial tax treatment could be concealed, the question is now at what amount the issue has to be accounted for. From the tax authorities' point of view, the assumption of a 100 percent detection risk is endorsed, since tax treatments with grave risks of non-acceptance are accounted for, about which the tax authorities may have been unaware previously. However, it is questionable to what extent German tax authorities can benefit from the relevant information in the IFRS financial statements. IFRIC 23 is a set of rules that applies to consolidated financial statements in accordance with IFRS (IASB, 2017, p. 5). In Germany, however, the individual financial statements in accordance with the German Commercial Code (HGB) form the basis for determining taxable profits (Herzig, 2004, p. 6). Since there is no principle of equal treatment of IFRS accounting and tax accounting (Kahle, Dahlke and Schulz, 2008, p. 513), and since tax authorities are only allowed to access data with tax relevance (Düren, 2007, p. 273), tax authorities are generally not authorized to view IFRS consolidated financial statements. Therefore, the extent to which tax auditors can view relevant information depends on how companies have organized their accounting. If commercial and tax accounting postings as well as IFRS adjustment postings that are tax-irrelevant are made in separate accounting areas, there is no possibility for the tax auditor to discern

IFRS values. If, however, adjustment postings are made in the same accounting area, a tax auditor can also identify alternative IFRS values. For this reason, companies no longer use this cancellation technique in practice.

Nevertheless, the extent to which companies are obligated to cooperate in explaining the provision for tax risks to tax auditors is disputed. According to the German Fiscal Code Application Decree (AEAO) to Sec. 200 AO, tax auditors have the right to request the audited consolidated financial statements of the parent company, the guidelines of the group parent company for the preparation of the consolidated financial statements and the consolidation-capable individual financial statements of the group parent company as well as the domestic and foreign individual companies. But even if the tax auditor makes use of this right, it is questionable to what extent he can draw relevant information from these documents. In the balance sheet and in the notes, potential additional claims by tax authorities for uncertain tax treatments are often not taken into account, as companies do not want to direct tax auditors to all disputed tax treatments that may not be discovered without disclosure (Walz, Briese and Haas, 2013, p. 170). The informative value of the reporting in the management report with regard to tax risks is very limited as well. Tax risks are often not listed in the opportunity and risk report or only described in general terms (Hoffmann, 2010, p. 239). This shows the crucial conflict of interest between tax authorities and companies. While tax authorities want to take up as much information as possible, companies do not want the tax auditor to come across all existing controversial tax treatments by providing too detailed information in the notes. In addition, companies do not want to give tax auditors any indication of the maximum amount up to which additional tax payments could exist at the company and should therefore be discovered by them. Moreover, the reporting companies are confronted with the conflict of interest between a true and fair presentation of the annual financial statements on the one hand and the disclosure of unrecognized tax items in the notes which indicates a future outflow of funds and a reduction in earnings on the other hand (Zion and Varshney, 2007, p. 1).

Although, according to IFRIC 23, tax treatments with a high probability of non-acceptance must be accounted for, the introduction of this provision will not significantly reduce companies' incentives to engage in aggressive tax avoidance activities. Companies seeking to use aggressive tax planning strategies will continue to exploit every tax loophole until the tax planning strategy used is classified to be aggressive and illegitimate. Before that, no company will draw attention to its tax strategy by reporting it as a tax risk. IFRIC 23 rather relates to tax uncertainties that arise from the legal application of tax law. Prior to IFRIC 23, every deviation in accounting from the tax return was declared as tax evasion. With the introduction of IFRIC 23, there was a change in perspective. Nowadays, a deviation does not immediately imply deliberate tax evasion, but arises from the fact that there is scope for the interpretation of tax law.

4.1.3 Solutions

In order to enable German tax authorities to benefit from IFRIC 23 as well, the reporting requirements for uncertain tax treatments should be extended beyond financial statements towards tax returns, following the US model. On January 26, 2010 the American tax administration IRS published the "Announcement 2010-09", according to which companies must declare uncertain tax positions recorded in the financial statements in an attachment to the corporate income tax return from the 2010 tax year (IRS, 2010a, p. 1). For this purpose, a tabular form "Schedule UTP (Form 1120)" was developed in which every uncertain tax position must be entered (IRS, 2019a, pp. 2–4). In addition to a concise description of the uncertain tax positions, the tabular form also contains mandatory fields for entering the relevant sections of the US Income Tax Act, the classification as permanent or temporary difference and the relevant tax years (IRS, 2019b, p. 2). Another mandatory indication is the maximum amount of the possible tax adjustment (IRS, 2019b, p. 3). However, companies are not required to report their own assessment of the tax position and the amount of the provisions recognized for each individual tax position (Risse, 2011, p. 670). Initially, only companies with USD 100 million in total assets were required to submit this form (IRS, 2010b, p. 4). During the five-year transition period, the asset threshold was lowered to USD 10 million to include smaller companies as well (IRS, 2010b, p. 4). German companies that have to prepare or are included in financial statements prepared in accordance with US GAAP or IFRS in the USA and have to submit a tax return in the USA are already affected by this reporting requirement (Walz et al., 2013, p. 172). The introduction of a corresponding obligation in Germany should therefore not be entirely new for certain German companies. Filing uncertain tax treatments in tax returns would improve the transparency of material tax issues and the efficiency of tax audits since auditors would then deal less with collecting documents and concentrate more on the actual audit. This would help to accelerate tax audits which would also be in the interest of companies.

To reduce the conflict of interest between tax authorities and companies, cooperative models are used in practice. The German tax authorities have implemented several pilot projects aimed at reforming the conventional tax audit. In this context, the Bielefeld model, Osnabrück model, NRW model and Bavarian model should be mentioned (Wünnemann, 2011, p. 198). Additionally, in Lower Saxony, a cooperatively aligned Group tax audit has been tested since 2012 (Kaiser, 2013, p. 1). In these models, companies are encouraged to voluntarily grant the tax authorities complete insight into all relevant information and to inform them of all tax treatments that pose a serious risk of divergent assessment by the tax authority, provided that significant effects on the tax result are expected (Hruschka, 2012, p. 4). They also need to explain how they manage and control tax risks (Hardeck, 2013, p. 158). In return, the tax authorities undertake to clarify the tax issues instantly and thus offer legal and planning security with regard to potential tax back payments (Birkemeyer, Blaufus, Keck, Reineke and Trenn, 2019, p. 121 et seq.). With this exchange of transparency for security, an intersection of interests can be found between companies and tax authorities. Cooperative tax auditing programs are also being implemented at international level. On January 23, 2018, the OECD launched the International Compliance Assurance Program (ICAP) (Prinz and Ludwig, 2018, p. 477). Due to constitutional concerns, Germany was only an observer in the pilot program, but is participating in the second phase, ICAP 2.0, which started on March 28, 2019 (Völk and Kobiella, 2019, p. 637). The aim of this program is to enable tax authorities and multinational companies to enter into an open dialogue about potential tax risks and to create legal and planning security through a multilateral and cooperative tax risk assessment (OECD, 2021, p. 6). ICAP 2.0 focuses in particular on tax risks in the context of transfer pricing, permanent establishments and other cross-border income tax issues such as withholding taxes, hybrid company structures and application of double tax treaties (OECD, 2021, p. 16 et seq.).

An effective combat against aggressive tax planning results from the coexistence of strict reporting and disclosure obligations, unilateral, bilateral and multilateral initiatives as well as fundamental tax law reforms. Unilateral interventions include, for example, a general anti-abuse regulation within the meaning of Sec. 42 AO (Haarmann, 2018, p. 561). The expansion of withholding taxes on interest and license payments could be mentioned as bilateral and multilateral measures (Fuest, Spengel, Finke, Heckemeyer and Nusser, 2013, p. 33). One example of a fundamental reform of tax law is the introduction of common global minimum tax rules (Altenburg, Geberth, Gebhardt, Holle and Oertel, 2019, p. 2451). However, in order to counteract aggressive tax planning, the concepts developed by the EU, OECD and G20 countries are of particular importance.

4.2 Perspective of Business Practice

4.2.1 Analysis of the Effect of the First-Time Application of IFRIC 23 on 2019 Consolidated Financial Statements

In the 2019 consolidated financial statements, IFRS accountants in Germany had to apply IFRIC 23 for the first time. Therefore, it is questionable whether the first-time application of this interpretation had a material impact on the presentation of the asset, financial and earnings position. To examine this, the consolidated financial statements as of December 31, 2019 are analyzed for the 30 companies listed in the DAX and the 60 companies listed in the MDAX at the end of December 2020. For companies whose fiscal year deviates from the calendar year, the 2018/2019 consolidated financial statements[1] or the 2019 consolidated financial statements[2] as the larger proportionate year are used. For Siemens Energy, the consolidated financial statement as of December 31, 2020 is used, as this is the first financial statement since the company was founded on April 1, 2020. The companies analyzed have provided the information on the first-time application of IFRIC 23 in separate sections of the annual report. Therefore, in addition to the section on the new standards and interpretations to be applied in the current financial year, the notes to income taxes are considered in the analysis. Moreover, the statements in the report on opportunities and risks of the group management report are included. The financial statements are analyzed with regard to the date of initial application, the transition method applied, the extent of reporting on initial application, the self-assessment of the materiality of the effects of initial application and the qualitative and quantitative information on the effects. Appendix G presents the results of this analysis.

The consolidated financial statements of the 90 companies examined show that 86 companies (96 %) applied IFRIC 23 for the first time on or after January 1, 2019, three companies (3 %) made use of the permitted earlier application of IFRIC 23 and for one company (1 %) the date of initial application could not be determined as it did not report any information about this provision. It is therefore questionable whether this company complies with the requirements on accounting for uncertain tax treatments.

In the consolidated financial statements analyzed, 87 companies (97 %) did not provide any information on the transition method used. Three companies (3 %) indicated that they used the modified retrospective approach, but none of

[1] See Aurubis, Carl Zeiss Meditec, Hella, Metro and Thyssenkrupp.

[2] See Gerresheimer, Infineon, Osram Licht, Siemens and Siemens Healthineers.

the companies (0 %) reported that they used the full retrospective approach. Information on the transition method was not required to be disclosed in the financial statements. Thus, companies did not voluntarily provide any information that goes beyond the legal obligations. However, for most companies, IFRIC 23 did not lead to any changes so that no adjustments were necessary. This is different for the three companies that provided information on the transition method. They preferred the modified retrospective approach over the full retrospective approach, which can be justified by the fact that the modified retrospective approach is less cumbersome as previous periods do not need to be restated.

Apart from one company (1 %), all of the companies examined provided information on the first-time application of IFRIC 23. With 46 companies (51 %), slightly more than half of the companies referred very briefly to the first-time application of IFRIC 23 in up to three sentences. The other half, consisting of 43 companies (48 %), explained the first-time application in detail on more than a quarter of a page. All companies that made brief statements assessed the impact of IFRIC 23 on the consolidated financial statement as immaterial. Whereas all companies that have classified the impact as material have provided comprehensive explanations. However, these explanations mainly contain a reproduction of the legal text or are limited to remarks on possible legislative amendments, the difficulties in enforcing one's own convictions of a tax treatment against the tax authorities and the complexity of tax law as a whole with its scope for different interpretations. The proportion of company-specific information, however, is low. In general, company-specific explanations can only be found in the financial statements of those companies that have quantified the effects of the first-time application of IFRIC 23 on the presentation of the consolidated financial statements. In the report on opportunities and risks, all sorts of risks relating to the economy as a whole, the industry, research and development, environmental protection, etc. are listed. However, taxes are rarely mentioned as a risk factor and if they are, it is stated that the management is in control of them. Therefore, the informative value of these extensive explanations is also limited.

Almost all of the companies examined (88 %) have classified the effects of the first-time application of IFRIC 23 on the presentation of the Group's asset, financial and earnings position as immaterial. Only three companies (3 %) rated the impact as material. The remaining eight companies (9 %) have not made a self-assessment with regard to the materiality. Thereby, it should be noted that a self-assessment of the materiality was not required to be disclosed in the notes. Those companies that stated that the first-time application of IFRIC 23 had no or only immaterial effects indirectly quantified the impact as zero. This was the case for 72 companies (80 %). Eight companies (9 %) have quantified the adjustment effects of the first-time application. Thereof, two companies have made a rough estimate, as they stated the effects would be in the two-digit and three-digit million range, and the other six companies have given specific values. One company (1 %) did not quantify the effects but described them qualitatively. The remaining nine companies (10 %) did not provide any information.

The adjustment effects arise for various reasons. The reason that was mentioned most frequently and caused high adjustment effects is that tax authorities may not accept a tax treatment. In particular, the possibility of not accepting the tax treatment of a liquidation loss (Beiersdorf, 2019, p. 104), lease structures (Lufthansa, 2019, p. 215), partial write-downs on shareholder loans (Lufthansa, 2019, p. 215), an acquisition of a foreign subsidiary (TeamViewer, 2019, p. 119) and transfer pricing issues (Dürr, 2019, p. 125) were mentioned. In addition, one company made adjustments because of an enacted foreign tax reform (Siemens Healthineers, 2019, p. 72). Another company had to make adjustments because it has used the virtually certain recognition threshold previously and now has to use the probable threshold (Lufthansa, 2019, p. 146). The second most common reason for the adjustments, but which do not affect the balance sheet items by amount, are reclassifications from income tax provisions to current income tax liabilities. Moreover, companies quantified the adjustment effects from the application of the transition method and the interest payments to tax authorities.

In summary, for the majority of the 90 companies examined, the first-time application of IFRIC 23 had little or no impact on the presentation of the asset, financial and earnings position. However, for those companies that experienced adjustment effects, the effects were significant.

4.2.2 Challenges

In order to investigate the difficulties encountered by companies in applying IFRIC 23, expert interviews were conducted with executives and employees who work in the corporate tax department of a DAX and MDAX company. The interview guide is attached in Appendix F. The key findings of the interviews are summarized in this and the following section.

Identifying tax risks is a major challenge for both large and small companies. Large corporations face various difficulties in this regard. The ongoing operational business results in less significant tax risks in quantitative and qualitative terms. In addition, these risks are monitored regularly. However, risks associated with group restructuring are very difficult to identify and monitor. In the case of a business acquisition, the problem is to discover the entire tax history of the acquired company. At the date of acquisition, the assets acquired and liabilities assumed are accounted for in accordance with IFRS 3. However, the accounting is only based on the company's best possible estimate at the date of the transfer of control. The actual tax risks existing in the acquired company can only be detected in the course of time. Therefore, the reality can only be grasped a couple of years later. However, the review by the tax authorities usually takes place after the time of purchase when the actual tax risks has not been captured yet.

In the case of an intragroup restructuring in which the existing parent-subsidiary relationship persists, the problem is to understand the complex and nested corporate structures implemented. Without a complete understanding of the group structure, many existing and potentially relevant tax risks will not be identified. In contrast to a company acquisition, tax risks resulting of such transactions are generally better documented and controlled since the subsidiary is under control of the parent company from the beginning. Nevertheless, large companies that are operating across borders are faced with a major challenge here.

In the case of a business disposal, the problem is that the selling company has to bear tax risks that arise after the date on which the control over the sold company was relinquished. In general, the buying company will always seek to transfer tax risks to the selling company that were not known at the date of disposal and that arise over time in the transferred company.

Compared to large companies, small but international companies do not have the tax expertise to identify and monitor tax risks. Although they have tax experts at their domestic headquarters, they do not have tax specialists at their foreign manufacturing plants and subsidiary sales companies. The domestic tax experts do not know which tax-relevant and potentially tax-dubious transactions are processed in the foreign companies. In addition, the sales employees do not have the expertise to assess the transactions for tax purposes and to forward relevant information to the headquarter. The problem for small companies is therefore the gathering and merging of information. As a result, many existing and potentially relevant tax risks are not taken into consideration.

Another problem area is uncertain tax treatments that affect deferred taxes. Prior to IFRIC 23, uncertainties of permanent nature and current taxes were already taken into account when assessing tax risks. However, uncertainties of temporary nature, deferred taxes and the interactions between current and deferred taxes were often neglected. With IFRIC 23, companies are now obliged to consider these as well. This has posed challenges for many companies as their monitoring and calculation efforts have increased and their accounting has changed. Deferred taxes arise not only in connection with temporary but also with permanent balance sheet differences. In the case of uncertainties in connection with temporary differences and a positive taxable income, the uncertainties have no tax effects, provided that deferred taxes are fully recoverable, due to the interactions between current and deferred taxes. In the case of a negative taxable income, the interactions usually take place entirely in the deferred taxes. Although the uncertainties increase or decrease the deferred tax assets on loss carryforwards, they have an opposite effect in the deferred taxes on temporary differences. In the case of uncertainties in connection with permanent differences and a negative taxable income, the amount of the tax loss carryforward changes so that the accounting for deferred taxes is affected as well.

Furthermore, the accounting for the effects of uncertainties on deferred taxes in the case of fiscal units poses several problems for companies. The first question is whether the effects of uncertainties on deferred taxes are calculated and accounted for at the level of the controlling company or each controlled company. In practice, two different approaches have become established. According to the formal approach, deferred taxes on temporary differences are recognized at the level of the controlling company for the entire income tax consolidation group (Lüdenbach et al., 2020, rec. 199). Whereas, according to the economic approach, the effects of uncertainties on deferred taxes are calculated separately for all companies in the fiscal unit (Lüdenbach et al., 2020, rec. 199). The second question is how pre-organizational temporary differences are accounted for. When applying the formal approach, they have to be resolved and then reassigned at the controlling company with its tax rate (Krimpmann, 2011, p. 76). When using the economic approach, the pre-organizational accounting on deferred taxes is retained (Krimpmann, 2011, p. 77). The third question is whether deferred tax assets can be recognized for pre-organizational losses. While pre-organizational losses of the controlling company remain fungible in the usual form, pre-organizational losses of the controlled companies cannot be used during the existence of the fiscal unit (Neumann, 2020, rec. 2). If a controlled company joins a fiscal unit, deferred taxes on loss carryforwards have to be written off through profit or loss (Pilhofer, Suermann and Müller, 2014, p. 160). If the company leaves the fiscal unit or the fiscal unit is dissolved, pre-organizational losses can be used again and deferred tax assets can be recognized if they are recoverable (Pilhofer et al., 2014, p. 160). The fourth question is how the recoverability of deferred tax assets resulting from deductible temporary differences has to be assessed. The controlled companies cannot assess the recoverability of their deferred tax assets in isolation, as the tax effect occurs at the level of the controlling company for the entire income tax consolidation group (Senger and Diersch, 2020, rec. 145). Therefore, the entire fiscal unit has to be taken into account when assessing the recoverability of a deferred tax asset (Senger and Diersch, 2020, rec. 145). As a result, a two-stage or multi-stage recoverability assessment has to be conducted, which can be very challenging.

The third major problem area is the accounting for interest and penalties in connection with uncertain tax treatments. With the DRSC Interpretation 4, the IFRS Committee of the DRSC stipulated that interest and penalties have to be accounted for in accordance with IAS 37 in Germany (DRSC, 2018, rec. 6). In the German legal system, they are not calculated on the basis of the taxable profit and consequently do not meet the definition of income taxes in IAS 12 (DRSC, 2018, rec. B5). The prohibition of the application of IAS 12 poses several difficulties for companies. First, tax back payments and related interest payments are often negotiated as a total amount in tax audits because it is difficult to separate taxes and interest when multiple tax years are assessed. Since a subsequent separation by companies is not possible, negotiations must be limited to the additional tax payment in future. Second, while according to IAS 37, the probable threshold applies to obligations arising from interest and penalties (DRSC, 2018, rec. 7), the virtually certain threshold applies to claims from interest and penalties (DRSC, 2018, rec. 9). This unequal treatment leads to income tax claims being recognized at an earlier stage than the related interest refund. Third, multinational companies tend to apply the accounting rules consistently within the group. Due to the regulation of the IFRS IC, there might be country-specific differences in the accounting for interest and penalties. Reflecting these differences adequately in the group tax reporting is a major challenge for companies.

4.2.3 Solutions

In order to ensure a comprehensive identification of tax risks and a uniform application of the requirements of IFRIC 23, small and large companies should formulate group-wide standards for the identification of and the accounting for tax risks in a group tax guideline and IFRS accounting guideline. In particular, rules should be developed for evaluating typical group restructuring transactions.

For large corporations that operate in different tax jurisdictions, it is advisable to integrate a web-based tax reporting tool with a questionnaire on tax risks into the IT infrastructure. The questionnaire can help to query and document tax risks globally in a standardized and centralized manner. The risks are recorded on a case-by-case basis at the level of the individual company with information on the probability of occurring and possible tax back payments. In the case of risks with a probability of occurring of more than 50 percent, the tax risk inventory also inquires whether the issue has a permanent or temporary effect on the tax calculation. As part of the query, the reported risks must be reassessed regarding new relevant facts or circumstances and changes in case law or administrative instructions. If risks no longer exist, they are deleted and recorded with the reason for deletion. Error messages also have to be documented in the questionnaire. The information recorded in the questionnaire is transferred directly to the group risk management system and the group tax department. The group tax de-partment manages the tax risks together with representatives of the legal department, financial and management accounting and internal audit. The tax risk inventory is carried out quarterly under observance of the dual control principle.

In order to minimize the tax risks associated with a company acquisition for the buyer, a tax due diligence should be conducted (Löffler, 2004, p. 576). As part of a tax due diligence, previous tax returns and tax audit reports of the company acquired must be examined regarding tax risks for the purchaser (Krüger and Kalbfleisch, 1999, p. 180). Thereby, statutory limitation periods need to be considered (Beisel, 2016, rec. 41). For the tax assessment periods that are still open, the buyer must conduct a tax audit by himself (Beisel, 2016, rec. 42). In the case of internal group restructurings, the underlying facts, restructuring steps and tax consequences should continuously be documented in memoranda. These can help to obtain a better overview of complex restructuring projects as well as to identify and weigh potential risks in advance. In order to minimize the tax risks associated with a company disposal for the seller, tax clauses should be included in the purchase agreement (Hülsmann, 2008, p. 2402). Although tax due diligence checks have been carried out in advance, it is not always possible to fully identify tax risks (Stümper and Walter, 2008, p. 32), which is why the remaining risks should be allocated to the contracting parties according to the principle of causation using tax clauses (Eilers and Beutel, 2010, p. 564). With tax clauses, statutory liability obligations can be limited or expanded by defining guarantee promises of the seller and exemption rights of the buyer (Bisle, 2013, p. 205).

For small companies, it is advisable to identify and monitor tax risks using classic spreadsheet programs. The tax risks can be entered into self-created detailed lists and viewed in an aggregated overview. Since the identification and monitoring of tax risks requires special knowledge and skills in operational risk management and taxation, those responsible for tax accounting and reporting should receive regular training. Auditing and tax advisory firms can also be commissioned to provide support on tax issues. Furthermore, small but international companies should set up tax hubs in the geographical areas in which they operate. The project teams in the tax hubs take care of the country-specific tax regulations, exchange information with the foreign tax authorities and forward tax-relevant information to the group tax department.

To ensure that deferred taxes are taken into account in addition to current taxes, the integration of a schedule of latency into the tax calculation tool is recommended. With a schedule of latency, the occurrence, development and reversal of temporary balance sheet differences can be shown (Krimpmann, 2011, p. 61). The balance sheet items on which the differences between commercial and tax book values are based as well as whether the differences lead to deferred tax assets or liabilities must be stated (Winnefeld, 2015, rec. 398). In addition, the amount of the respective differences and the tax rates with which the measurement is carried out should be specified (Krimpmann, 2011, p. 61). The period or the point in time at which the temporary differences will reverse should also be stated (Bantleon and Schorr, 2010, p. 1492). In the case of a fiscal unit, the application of the economic approach requires not only the creation of a schedule of latency for the controlling company but also for the controlled companies (Winnefeld, 2015, rec. 395). When applying the formal approach, only a schedule of latency for the controlling company is required (Winnefeld, 2015, rec. 395). If there is a tax loss carryforward and there are uncertainties for prior periods, the further development of the tax loss carryforward should be presented in a shadow calculation that takes into account the effects of the uncertainties (Jacob and Kazuch, 2018, p. 209). In a shadow calculation, the tax calculations for the current financial year and for all open years in the past are mirrored in a second version based on the tax returns and are supplemented by the effects from the assessment of the uncertainties (Kämpfer, 2017, p. 458). Shadow calculations can take into account complex tax situations with all consequences and interactions resulting from the uncertainties (Kämpfer, 2017, p. 458).

In order to facilitate the separation of interest payments from tax payments when negotiation packages were agreed during the tax audit, IT applications for simulating tax audits can be used. Tax audit simulations offer the possibility to calculate complex tax effects and to determine tax surpluses or reductions. The resulting interest payments are then automatically computed by the software according to the regulations of Sec. 233a AO. In addition, such software solutions enable the integration of the different recognition thresholds of IAS 37 for claims and obligations. Furthermore, by integrating other country-specific regulations and national interest rates, tax audits abroad can also be simulated.

4.3 Perspective of Advisory Practice

4.3.1 Analysis of the FREP Results of the 2020 Audit

Each year, ESMA defines European common enforcement priorities which European enforcers should consider when auditing annual financial statements of listed companies. In the light of the first-time mandatory application of IFRIC 23 for fiscal years beginning on or after January 1, 2019, the proper application of this interpretation is one of the key topics in the 2020 audit season (ESMA, 2019, p. 1). The FREP, as the national enforcer in Germany, has adopted the key audit areas of ESMA and will therefore pay particular attention to the application of IFRIC 23 in the 2019 IFRS financial statements of listed companies in Germany (FREP, 2019, p. 1). In addition to the correct accounting of these new requirements, ESMA emphasizes the need to make assumptions and estimates as well as the discretionary decisions and the accounting methods transparent to financial statement users (ESMA, 2019, p. 8). In particular, it must be stated whether uncertain tax treatments were considered separately or together and whether the expected value approach or the most likely amount approach was used (Bischof, Link and Staß, 2020, p. 5). Moreover, ESMA notes that uncertain tax assets and liabilities must be reported as current or deferred taxes and that it is not permitted to include them in other provisions (Beyhs, 2019, p. 520).

In 2020, the FREP performed 74 audits, of which 66 were randomly selected, three were indication-based and five were requested by the BaFin (FREP, 2020, p. 2). Erroneous accounting was found in eleven audits, which corresponds to an error rate of 15 percent (FREP, 2020, p. 9). The errors identified are essentially caused by difficulties in applying IFRS with regard to complex business transactions and the incomplete reporting in the notes and management report (FREP, 2020, p. 13). However, no incorrect accounting with regard to IFRIC 23 could be identified in the audit procedures performed (FREP, 2020, p. 19).

Since IFRIC 23 was one of the key audit areas of ESMA and FREP in the 2020 audit season, companies, together with their auditors, evaluated the uncertainties contained in their tax returns and reflected them in the 2019 financial statements in accordance with the new regulation. To investigate the challenges auditors faced with regard to IFRIC 23, expert interviews were conducted with auditors from two large auditing firms. The interview guide is attached in Appendix F.

4.3.2 Challenges

Auditors were particularly faced with the challenge of clarifying the differences between FIN 48 and IFRIC 23 to companies that have prior knowledge of FIN 48 and prepare their financial statements in accordance with both IFRS and US GAAP. Although the same uncertain tax positions are reported in the US GAAP and IFRS financial statements, the application of FIN 48 and IFRIC 23 leads to different results due to different recognition and measurement requirements. This fact is often not understood by internal tax experts, financial analysts and shareholders. From their point of view, different results on the same issue reduce the credibility of financial statements. The enforcement authorities, on the other hand, carefully check whether such GAAP differences are captured by companies and are adequately reflected in their accounting. Compared to US companies, German companies have great difficulties in applying this regulation. There are two reasons for this. First, US companies have a twelve-year head start when it comes to accounting for uncertain tax positions and second, the separation between the financial accounting department and the tax department is more pronounced in German companies than in US companies. In Germany, the tax accounting processes are often performed in the financial accounting department and not in the tax department (Meyer, 2018, p. 863). The most important tasks of a company's tax department include preparing tax returns, ensuring tax compliance, managing tax risks and planning taxes (Rose, 1968, p. 36). Whereas, it is the responsibility of the financial accounting department to ensure that the financial statements convey a true and fair view (Baetge, Kirsch and Thiele, 2019, p. 151). Therefore, the linkage between the process of preparing tax returns and the accounting is particularly problematic (Herzig, 2010, p. 6).

The accounting for uncertain tax treatments is largely based on subjective assessments by the reporting company. The scope of discretion enables a wide range of acceptable valuation approaches, whose limits cannot be objectively defined. In addition, there is often a lack of adequate internal determination and documentation. The challenge for auditors is therefore to assess whether the discretionary decisions are traceable and plausible. Scope of discretion exists at many decision-making levels, for example in the definition of the unit of account, the assessment of whether the recognition threshold has been reached and the application of the measurement approaches. IFRIC 23 specifies how to proceed when determining the unit of account. Nevertheless, there is certain scope of discretion in assessing the level of aggregation. Companies try to take advantage of this and disaggregate the unit of account in order to adhere the recognition threshold, although the entire unit of account would exceed the recognition threshold and lead to the recognition of the uncertain tax position. The decision as to whether the recognition threshold is reached or not is also subject to discretion. The reporting companies are faced with the challenge of assessing whether it is more likely than not that the tax authorities will accept the tax treatment. This decision cannot be made on purely objective criteria and without hindsight. Companies will only find out retrospectively whether the tax authorities will accept the tax treatment. Furthermore, the measurement methods provided by IFRIC 23 depend on subjective assessments by the reporting company. Tax experts do not find it difficult to determine the possible outcomes of a tax uncertainty but to estimate the exact probabilities of occurrence of each outcome. Statistical data for the probability estimations is not available as uncertain tax treatments are often unique. Moreover, no information is known about comparable cases due to the tax secrecy. Consequently, the broad scope of discretion can be used in such a way that will not lead to a more conservative accounting for uncertain tax treatments. Further, companies have the tendency to change the accounting policy adopted even though no new information is available, or new information is available but not taken into account.

In addition, IFRIC 23 can further exacerbate the tension between auditing and tax advisory services. The auditor can be confronted with the contradicting decision as to whether he should demand an increase in tax expenses during an audit if he or his audit firm has recommended the underlying tax treatment in connection with a tax advice (Kovermann and Velte, 2017, p. 409). This conflict does not exist in the case of public interest companies, since Sec. 605 of the IESBA Code of Ethics, Art. 5 of the EU Statutory Audit Directive and Sec. 319a Para. 1 No. 2 HGB prohibit the provision of tax advisory services to audit clients (Klaas, 2014, p. 763). The reason for this is that the auditor's independency is endangered due to the self-review (Lanfermann, 2014, p. 1771). Non-public interest companies, however, are not affected by these regulations (Klaas, 2014, p. 763). It is therefore doubtful whether the auditor will objectively examine his own proposals and admit that he may have provided inadequate advice.

4.3.3 Solutions

In practice, GAAP differences are resolved in such a way that the accountant initially calculates correctly according to both the US GAAP regulations and IFRS regulations. The calculations are then adjusted until the same result is obtained. As a result, sometimes the US GAAP approach and sometimes the IFRS approach is correct, or both approaches are incorrect. The correct result will only be known ex post. To make companies and especially those interested in the financial statements more aware of the differences between FIN 48 and IFRIC 23, the existing differences in accounting between the US GAAP and IFRS regulations need to receive more attention in the relevant literature (KPMG, 2017, p. 1). In addition, the FASB and IASB convergence project to harmonize the accounting standards should be continued (Ong, 2018, p. 101 et seq.). Moreover, the accounting regulations on income taxes should be simplified as income taxes are a very complex and challenging accounting area (FASB, 2019, p. 1).

In order to facilitate the plausibility check of the company's discretionary decisions, it is advisable that audit firms provide companies with an IFRIC 23 solution with which the standard-compliant application can be documented and internal value determinations as well as the reasons for the discretionary decisions can be presented. Such an IFRIC 23 solution improves the transparency of financial statements as required by ESMA and helps to achieve a more effective and efficient audit of financial statements. In order to ensure that the unit of account is defined as reasonably and objectively as possible, each audit finding contained in a tax audit report should form a unit of account, as this is the level of aggregation at which the tax authority makes its assessment (Ruberg, 2017, p. 249). Even if the number and the scope of audit findings are not known to companies in advance, they can refer to their previous experience with tax audits and the scope of their audit findings in the past. To prevent the probability estimates from being arbitrary when assessing whether the recognition threshold has been reached, a panel of tax experts with different attitudes should be consulted to estimate the probability that the tax authorities will or will not accept the tax treatment (Blaufus, Bob and Trinks, 2013, p. 2). The advantage of this is that overly optimistic and overly pessimistic estimates offset each other, and thus more accurate estimates are provided. Alternatively, the estimation of bandwidths in a first step could also help to determine an exact probability in a second step by limiting the bandwidth (Lawsky, 2009, p. 1071). These two methods can also be used when measuring the tax uncertainty using the most likely amount method in order to determine the probabilities of occurrence of the two possible outcomes. To ensure that no randomly distributed probabilities are determined when applying the expected value method, companies should implement a methodical procedure for determining the probabilities of occurrence (Hafkenscheid and Janssen, 2009, p. 41). For this purpose, all relevant scenarios and their possible outcomes have to be presented in a decision table (Hafkenscheid and Janssen, 2009, p. 42). In addition, the conditions on which the scenarios are based have to be recorded in sub tables (Hafkenscheid and Janssen, 2009, p. 42). In this way, scenarios can be compared and related to one another (Hafkenscheid and Janssen,

2009, p. 42). The scenarios then have to be weighted at each decision level with their probability of occurrence (Hafkenscheid and Janssen, 2009, p. 42). To what extent the implementation of such a subdivided methodical process makes sense, taking the cost-benefit ratio into account, remains unclear. In addition, subjective assessments ultimately flow into every decision level which either compensate or accumulate to the wrong decision. Ex ante, tax experts will never be able to determine the exact cash outflow. The audit of current and deferred taxes has already been a very demanding audit area in the past (Loitz, 2012, p. 247). With IFRIC 23, auditors are even more likely to require the assistance of tax advisors when conducting audits (Loitz, 2012, p. 254).

The trade-off between auditing and tax advice, which is reinforced by IFRIC 23, can, however, reduce aggressive tax behavior if auditing and tax advisory services are offered by a single provider (Kovermann and Velte, 2017, p. 409). This relationship is also confirmed empirically. Klassen et al. (2016) provide evidence that, in the US, companies that hire their auditor to prepare their tax returns claim less aggressive tax positions than companies that prepare their own tax returns or hire an external tax advisor. In addition, Watrin, Burggraef and Weiß (2019) find that, in Germany, auditor-provided tax services reduce corporate tax avoidance and are related to more conservative tax strategies. However, the empirical studies do not present a uniform picture as some studies also find a positive relationship between auditor-provided tax services and tax avoidance. Hogan and Noga (2015), for example, show that tax advisory services provided by the auditor increase tax avoidance due to knowledge spillover effects.

Conclusion

5

The objective of this thesis was to examine the differences between FIN 48 and IFRIC 23 as well as the practical effects of IFRIC 23 on the tax authority, business and advisory practice in Germany. The comparison of FIN 48 and IFRIC 23 shows that the similarities lie primarily in the objectives of the interpretations and the motivation for issuing them. General similarities can further be identified in the personal and temporal scope, the unit of account, the detection risk as well as the treatment of changed facts and circumstances. Slight differences were discovered in the material scope, the treatment of subsequent events and the balance sheet presentation. The major differences, however, lie in the core of the accounting regulations, namely in the recognition and measurement regulations as well as the disclosure requirements. The inverse question structure in the recognition step shows the conceptual difference in the methodology for accounting for uncertain tax positions of the FASB and IASB. Significant practical consequences result from the different measurement methods according to FIN 48 and IFRIC 23, since different amounts are recorded for the same tax situation depending on the method applied. Moreover, IFRIC 23 stipulates far fewer disclosure requirements than FIN 48. In summary, it can be said that despite the convergence project of the FASB and IASB, different accounting concepts for uncertain tax positions were established under US GAAP and IFRS.

The expert interviews conducted show that IFRIC 23 is associated with a large variety of challenges in practice. The German tax authority cannot benefit from the information on uncertain tax positions in the financial statements as these are not sufficiently transparent. From the perspective of the business practice, IFRIC 23 significantly exacerbates the accounting difficulties associated with special accounting and tax topics, such as the accounting for deferred taxes in connection with fiscal units, and raises numerous further accounting questions. For the advisory practice, the challenge associated with IFRIC 23 is in particular

C. Seibert, *Differences between FIN 48 and IFRIC 23*, BestMasters,
https://doi.org/10.1007/978-3-658-39041-9_5

to check the plausibility of the discretionary decisions made by companies in the recognition and measurement step. To sum up, it can be said that even if the legal loophole on accounting for uncertain tax positions in IFRS has been closed, many practical application and objectification problems have arisen in connection with IFRIC 23. Overall, the results of this thesis demonstrate that uncertain tax positions significantly increase the complexity of tax accounting.

The chosen method of a qualitative interview has proven to be suitable. The interview method offered the opportunity to ask open-ended questions and to adjust the order of the questions individually. In addition, it was possible to explain questions and ask reciprocal questions on unclear issues. A critical point, however, is that the number of interviews was small and the choice of the interview partners was selective so that only a few views of the three parties could be reflected. As an alternative or supplementary method, group discussions might have been useful. In these, the interviewees could have mentioned further aspects through the mutual exchange. It should further be noted that the findings from the analysis of the 2019 financial statements are not necessarily representative of all IFRS reporters in Germany due to the deliberate selection of companies. The results only describe tendencies. To confirm them, the annual reports of small and medium-sized companies should also be analyzed.

Further normative research is required with regard to the differences between the accounting for uncertain tax positions according to international and national accounting standards. In particular for German companies, it is important to understand the differences between HGB, IFRS and US GAAP. In addition, it would be interesting to examine the extent to which the US accounting regulations influence the German accounting regulations. Due to the convergence project of the FASB and IASB, US regulations affect the IFRS regulation and these in turn influence the German regulations through the EU endorsement process. Additional empirical research is required regarding the impact of IFRIC 23 on the effective tax rate, as any recognition and release of a provision for uncertain tax positions will impact the annual effective tax rate in the financial statements. Studies are also required on the impact of IFRIC 23 on tax avoidance, earnings management and investor behavior.

As accounting standards and tax legislations are constantly evolving, their interdependencies are also changing. In consequence, accounting practice is becoming increasingly complex and challenging. It remains to be seen how far the disclosure obligations will go in the context of financial statements and tax declarations. For companies, it is becoming increasingly important to analyze and monitor uncertain tax positions, not only because of their risk potential, but also because of the constantly growing documentation and disclosure requirements.

References

Normative References

AICPA, Practice Guide on Accounting for Uncertain Tax Positions under FIN 48, 2006, available at: http://docplayer.net/59884799-American-institute-of-certified-public-accountants-practice-guide-on-accounting-for-uncertain-tax-positions-under-fin-48.html, accessed on October 15, 2020 at 8:55 a.m.

ALLTIZER, RICHARD L./MCALLISTER, BRIAN P./JARNAGIN, BILL D., FIN 48: Accounting and Auditing Implications, in: The CPA Journal, 2008, Vol. 78, No. 8, pp. 44–47.

ALTENBURG, NADIA/GEBERTH, GEORG/GEBHARDT, RONALD/HOLLE, FLORIAN/OERTEL, EVA, Pläne zur Einführung einer internationalen Mindestbesteuerung – Ein Überblick, in: DStR, 2019, pp. 2451–2458.

ANDREOLI, BRIAN E./COLKER, DAVID/LEBOVITZ, MICHAEL S., Legal and Practical Issues in Applying FIN 48, in: The Tax Executive, 2007, Vol. 59, No. 1, pp. 43–48.

BAETGE, JÖRG/KIRSCH, HANS-JÜRGEN/THIELE, STEFAN, Bilanzen, 15th edition, Düsseldorf 2019.

BANTELON, ULRICH/SCHORR, GERHARD, Ausgewählte Auswirkungen des BilMoG auf die Beurteilung der Kapitaldienstfähigkeit von nicht kapitalmarktorientierten Kapitalgesellschaften, in: DStR, 2010, pp. 1491–1497.

BEISEL, WILHELM, Sec. 2, Due Diligence, in: Der Unternehmenskauf, published by Beisel, Wilhelm/Klumpp, Hans-Hermann, 7th edition, Munich 2016.

BEYHS, OLIVER, Schwerpunkte des DPR-Enforcements der Finanzberichterstattung in 2020 – Worauf sich kapitalmarktorientierte Unternehmen diesmal einstellen müssen, in: IRZ, 2019, pp. 521–527.

BIRKEMEYER, ELLEN/BLAUFUS, KAY/KECK, SERJOSCHA/REINEKE, JAKOB/TRENN, ILKO, Kooperative Tax Compliance-Programme: Ein internationaler Vergleich (Teil I), in: DStR, 2019, pp. 121–127.

BISCHOF, STEFAN/LINK, ROBERT/STAß, ALEXANDER, DPR-Prüfungsschwerpunkte 2020, in: DB, 2020, pp. 1–8.

C. Seibert, *Differences between FIN 48 and IFRIC 23*, BestMasters, https://doi.org/10.1007/978-3-658-39041-9

BISLE, MICHAEL, Steuerklauseln in Unternehmenskaufverträgen, in: SteuK, 2013, pp. 204–207.

BMF, Ergebnisse der steuerlichen Betriebsprüfung 2019, 2020b, available at: https://www.bundesfinanzministerium.de/Monatsberichte/2020/10/Inhalte/Kapitel-3-Analysen/3-4-steuerliche-betriebspruefung-2019-pdf.pdf?_blob=publicationFile&v=5, accessed on February 5, 2021 at 9:10 a.m.

BMF, Statistik über die Einspruchsbearbeitung in den Finanzämtern im Jahr 2019, 2020a, available at: https://www.bundesfinanzministerium.de/Content/DE/Standardartikel/Themen/Steuern/Weitere_Steuerthemen/Abgabeordnung/BMF_Anordnungen_Allgemeines/2020–10–27-statistik-ueber-die-einspruchsbearbeitung-in-den-finanzaemtern-im-jahr-2019-anlage.pdf?__blob=publicationFile&v=2, accessed on February 5, 2021 at 9:00 a.m.

BRAZZIL, ROBERT E./STEIN, RONALD A., FIN 48 and IRS Settlements, in: The Insurance Tax Review, 2007, pp. 565–570.

BROWNE, JAMES R., Financial Reporting for Uncertain Tax Positions, in: The Insurance Tax Review, 2005, pp. 968–984.

COHEN, BRETT/MICHELUZZI, RETO, Lifting the Fog: Accounting for Uncertainty in Income Taxes, in: Tax Notes, 2006, pp. 233–236.

DAHLKE, JÜRGEN, Mehr Transparenz bei der Bilanzierung von Steuerrisiken?, in: KoR, 2007, p. 311–322.

DELOITTE, IFRIC 23: Uncertainty over income tax treatment, 2018, available at: https://www2.deloitte.com/content/dam/Deloitte/nl/Documents/tax/deloitte-nl-ifrs-23-tax-accounting-alert.pdf, accessed on October 15, 2020 at 10:00 a.m.

DELOITTE, Uncertainty in Income Taxes – A Roadmap to Applying Interpretation 48, 2007, available at: http://www.iasplus.com/en/publications/migrated/pub1487, accessed on October 15, 2020 at 9:00 a.m.

DETTMER, STEFFEN/HEINTGES, SEBASTIAN, Ertragsteuerliche Risiken und Chancen in der Bilanz? Wahrscheinliche immer!, in: WPg, 2016, pp. 79–85.

DONOHUE, MICHAEL J./LOWELL, CYM H./MARTIN, MARK R., Application of FIN 48 to Transfer Pricing and Permanent Establishment Issues, in: The Tax Executive, 2007, Vol. 59, No. 6, pp. 485–495.

DRSC, Accounting for Interest and Penalties Related to Income Taxes under IFRSs, 2018, available at: https://www.drsc.de/app/uploads/2018/07/180716_E-Interpretation_IFRS_1_en.pdf, accessed on February 20, 2021 at 3:15 p.m.

DRÜEN, KLAUS-DIETER, Neue Pflichten zur Vorlage von Unterlagen bei der Betriebsprüfung von Kapitalgesellschaften und Konzernen?, in: Steuerberater-Jahrbuch 2006/2007, published by Piltz, Detlev J./Günkel, Manfred/Niemann, Ursula, Cologne 2007, pp. 273–314.

EILERS, STEPHAN/BEUTEL, DAVID, Seminar G: Steuerfreistellungen und -gewährleistungen in M&A-Transaktionen, in: IStR, 2010, pp. 564–566.

EPSTEIN, BARRY J./NACH, RALPH/BRAGG, STEVEN M., Wiley GAAP 2008: Interpretation and Application of Generally Accepted Accounting Principles, 5th edition, New York 2007.

ESMA, European common enforcement priorities for 2019 annual financial reports, 2019, available at: https://www.esma.europa.eu/sites/default/files/library/esma32–63–791_esma_european_common_enforcement_priorities_2019.pdf, accessed on February 28, 2021 at 8:30 a.m.

ETPF, Measuring corporation tax uncertainty: Evidence from three phases of a cross-country survey, 2020, available at: https://files.taxfoundation.org/20201102135554/1-Measuring-Corporation-Tax-Uncertainty.pdf, accessed on November 10, 2020 at 4:30 p.m.

EY, Uncertainty over income tax treatments, 2017, available at: https://assets.ey.com/content/dam/ey-sites/ey-com/en_gl/topics/ifrs/ey-apply-income-taxes-november-2017.pdf?download, accessed on October 15, 2020 at 10:00 a.m.

FASB, Accounting Standards Codification: Notice to Contituents (v 3.0) About the Codification, 2009, available at: https://asc.fasb.org/imageRoot/32/6737032.pdf, accessed on October 15, 2020 at 10:00 a.m.

FASB, FASB Interpretation No. 48 – Accounting for Uncertainty in Income Taxes: an interpretation of FASB Statement No. 109, 2006, available at: https://www.fasb.org/jsp/FASB/Document_C/DocumentPage?cid=1218220134210&acceptedDisclaimer=true, accessed on October 7, 2020 at 9:30 a.m.

FASB, Income Taxes (Topic 740) Simplifying the Accounting for Income Taxes, 2019, available at: https://www.fasb.org/jsp/FASB/Document_C/DocumentPage?cid=1176173929469a&acceptedDisclaimer=true, accessed on March 2, 2021 at 3:30 p.m.

FASB, Statement of Financial Accounting Standards No. 109, 1992, available at: https://www.fasb.org/jsp/FASB/Document_C/DocumentPage?cid=1218220123761a&acceptedDisclaimer=true, accessed on October 15, 2020, 11:00 a.m.

FLÜCHTER, KARSTEN, Seminar C: Verständigungsverfahren und die Beilegung grenzüberschreitender Streitigkeiten, in: IStR, 2012, pp. 694–703.

FREP, Activity Report 2020, 2021, available at: https://www.frep.info/docs/jahresberichte/2020/2020_tb_en.pdf, accessed on February 28, 2021 at 8:40 a.m.

FREP, Enforcement priorities for 2020, 2019, available at: https://www.frep.info/docs/pressemitteilungen/2019/20191118_pm_en.pdf, accessed on February 28, 2021 at 8:35 a.m.

FRINK, EVELYN, Verständigungs- und Schiedsverfahren im Internationalen Steuerrecht, Trier 2015.

FUEST, CLEMENS/SPENGEL, CHRISTOPH/FINKE, KATHARINA/HECKEMEYER, JOST H./NUSSER, HANNAH, Handlungsoptionen gegen aggressive Steuerplanung, in: DB, 2013, pp. 33–36.

GAROFALO, WILLIAM/VALENTE, MARK, Measuring Tax Benefits under FIN 48 – Eliminating Some of the Agita, in: The Tax Executive, 2007, Vol. 59, No. 1, pp. 49–53.

GLOTH, THOMAS/LÜDDERS, MARC, IFRIC 23 „Unsicherheiten bei der ertragsteuerlichen Behandlung", in: DB, 2017, pp. 1857–1858.

HAARMANN, WILHELM, Die Missbrauchsverwirrung, in: IStR, 2018, pp. 561–574.

HAFKENSCHEID, RUTGER/JANSSEN, CLAUDIA, IAS 12 needs methodical approach., in: International Tax Review, 2009, Vol. 20, No. 2, pp. 41–43.

HARDECK, INGA, Kooperative Compliance Programme zwischen Finanzverwaltungen und Unternehmen – Zukunft oder Sackgasse? Eine international vergleichende Analyse, in: StuW, 2013, pp. 156–172.

HENNIG, CHERIE J./RAABE, WILLIAM A./EVERETT, JOHN O., FIN 48 Compliance: Disclosing Tax Positions in an Age of Uncertainty, in: The Tax Adviser, 2008, Vol. 2, No. 1, pp. 24–36.

HERZIG, NORBERT, BilMoG, Tax Accounting und Corporate Governance-Aspekte, in: DB, 2010, pp. 1–8.

HERZIG, NORBERT, IAS/IFRS und steuerliche Gewinnermittlung – Eigenständige Steuerbilanz und modifizierte Überschussrechnung, Gutachten für das Bundesfinanzministerium, Düsseldorf 2004.

HERZIG, NORBERT/HEIMIG, MICHAEL/VOSSEL, STEPHAN, Risikoorientiertes Tax Accounting nach ED/2009/2, in: DB, 2009, pp. 2613–2620.

HERZIG, NORBERT/LIEKENBROCK, BERNHARD, Bilanzierung von Steuerrückstellungen nach BilMoG und IDW RS HFA 34, in: DB, 2013, pp. 409–417.

HEY, JOHANNA, Steuerplanungssicherheit als Rechtsproblem, Cologne 2002.

HOFFMANN, WOLF-DIETER, Steuerrisiken, in: PiR, 2010, pp. 238–240.

HOLZMANN, OSCAR J./ROBINSON, TOM, FIN 48: Uncertain Tax Positions, in: The Journal of Corporate Accounting & Finance, 2007, Vol. 18, No. 3, pp. 87–90.

HRUSCHKA, FRANZ, Ausgewählte Aspekte der Betriebsprüfung, in: Stbg, 2012, pp. 1–6.

HÜLSMANN, MATTHIAS, Die Steuerklausel im Unternehmenskaufvertrag, in: DStR, 2008, pp. 2402–2407.

IASB, Comparison of different measures, 2011, available at: https://cdn.ifrs.org/-/media/feature/meetings/2011/february/iasb/cc-0211b02aobs.pdf, accessed on October 15, 2020 at 10:00 a.m.

IASB, Draft IFRIC Interpretation: Uncertainty overIncome Tax Treatments, 2015, available at: https://cdn.ifrs.org/-/media/project/uncertainty-over-income-tax-treatments/draft-interpretation/published-documents/di-uncertainty-income-tax-treatments.pdf, accessed on October 15, 2020 at 10:00 a.m.

IASB, IASB Update September 2002, 2002, available at: https://cdn.ifrs.org/-/media/feature/news/updates/iasb/2002/sep02.pdf, accessed on October 15, 2020 at 10:00 a.m.

IASB, IFRIC 23 Uncertainty over Income Tax Treatments, 2017, available at: http://eifrs.ifrs.org/eifrs/bnstandards/en/IFRIC23.pdf, accessed on October 15, 2020 at 10:00 a.m.

IASB, Measurement of current income tax on uncertain tax position, 2014b, available at: https://cdn.ifrs.org/-/media/feature/meetings/2014/september/ifrs-ic/ias-12-income-taxes/ap4-measurement-of-utp.pdf, accessed on October 15, 2020 at 10:00 a.m.

IASB, Presentation of Liabilities or Assets Related to Uncertain Tax Treatments, 2019, available at: https://cdn.ifrs.org/-/media/project/presentation-of-liabilities-or-assets-related-to-uncertain-tax-treatments/ias-1-presentation-of-liabilities-or-assets-related-to-uncertain-tax-treatments-september-2019.pdf, accessed on October 15, 2020 at 10:00 a.m.

IASB, Recognition of current income tax on uncertain tax position – Principles of the draft Interpretation, 2014a, available at: https://cdn.ifrs.org/-/media/feature/meetings/2014/july/ifrs-ic/ias-12-income-taxes/ap3-principles-of-interpretation.pdf, accessed on October 15, 2020 at 10:00 a.m.

IASB, Scope of the income tax project, 2009, available at: https://cdn.ifrs.org/-/media/feature/meetings/2009/november/joint-iasb-fasb/intax-1109-ap8-obs.pdf, accessed on October 15, 2020 at 10:00 a.m.

IASB/FASB, Short-term convergence: income taxes – uncertain tax positions (Agenda Paper 4A), 2005, available at: https://cdn.ifrs.org/-/media/feature/meetings/2005/october/jointiasbfasb/income-taxes-uncertain-tax-positions/ap4a-cover-note.pdf, accessed on October 15, 2020 at 10:00 a.m.

IESBA, Handbook of the International Code of Ethics for Professional Accountants, 2020, available at: https://www.ifac.org/system/files/publications/files/IESBA-English-2020-IESBA-Handbook_Web-LOCKED.pdf, accessed on February 28, 2021 at 5:30 p.m.

IFRS FOUNDATION, Who uses IFRS Standards?, 2020, available at: https://www.ifrs.org/use-around-the-world/use-of-ifrs-standards-by-jurisdiction/, accessed on October 15, 2020 at 10:00 a.m.

IRS, Announcement 2010-75, 2010b, available at: https://www.irs.gov/pub/irs-drop/a-10-75.pdf, accessed on February 11, 2021 at 4:25 p.m.

IRS, Announcement 2010-9, 2010a, available at: https://www.irs.gov/pub/irs-drop/a-10-09.pdf, accessed on February 11, 2021 at 3:45 p.m.

IRS, Instructions for Schedule UTP (Form 1120), 2019b, available at: https://www.irs.gov/pub/irs-pdf/i1120utp.pdf, accessed on February 11, 2021 at 4:20 p.m.

IRS, Schedule UTP (Form 1120), 2019a, available at: https://www.irs.gov/pub/irs-pdf/f1120utp.pdf, accessed on February 11, 2021 at 4:15 p.m.

JACOB, ANDREA/KAZUCH, ANNA, IFRIC 23: Unsicherheiten bei der Bilanzierung von Ertragsteuern nach IAS 12, in: WPg, 2018, pp. 208–213.

KAHLE, HOLGER/DAHLKE, ANDREAS/SCHULZ, SEBASTIAN, Die Bedeutung der IFRS für die Unternehmensbesteuerung vor dem Hintergrund aktueller Rechtsentwicklungen, in: IRZ, 2008, pp. 513–520.

KAISER, ANDREAS, Die kooperativ ausgerichtete Konzernbetriebsprüfung in Niedersachsen, in: StBp, 2013, pp. 1–4.

KÄMPFER, NILS, Praxis-Leitfaden zur Bilanzierung von Ertragsteuern bei Unsicherheiten nach IFRIC 23, in: IRZ, 2017, pp. 453–460.

KESSLER, WOLFGANG/SCHOLZ-GÖRLACH, ULRICH, ED/2009/2 Income Tax – Fortbestehende Unterschiede bei der Abbildung steuerrechtlicher Risiken zwischen US-GAAP und IFRS, in: PiR, 2009, pp. 285–290.

KIMMELFIELD, NEIL D./HOROWITZ, LEWIS M./DAVIS, PAIGE L., Accounting for Uncertainty in Income Taxes – The Effect of FASB Interpretation No. 48, in: The Tax Executive, 2006, Vol. 58, No. 4, pp. 292–299.

KLAAS, HELMUT, Steuerberatung gegenüber Prüfungsmandanten – Eine nach wie vor zulässige Dienstleistung auch bei Unternehmen von öffentlichem Interesse?, in: WPg, 2014, pp. 763–766.

KLOOSTERHOF, SANDER/van ZOELEN, DENNIS, International – Accounting for Uncertain Income Tax Positions, in: European Taxation, 2009, Vol. 49, No. 8/9, pp. 415–421.

KOVERMANN, JOST/VELTE, PATRICK, IFRIC 23 – Mehr Sicherheit in der Bilanzierung von Ertragsteuern nach IAS 12, in: IRZ, 2017, pp. 405–409.

KPMG, Accounting for Uncertainty in Income Taxes under IFRS and U.S. GAAP, 2017, available at: https://assets.kpmg/content/dam/kpmg/us/pdf/2017/10/tnf-wnit-gaap.pdf, accessed on October 15, 2020 at 10:00 a.m.

KPMG, Tax uncertainties in the United States, 2018, available at: https://advisory.kpmg.us/content/dam/frv/en/pdfs/2018/ifrs-tax-uncertainties-in-the-us.pdf, accessed on October 15, 2020 at 10:00 a.m.

KRIMPMANN, ANDREAS, Latente Steuern in der Praxis, Freiburg 2011.

KRÖNER, MICHAEL/BECKENHAUB, CLAUS, Konzernsteuerquote: Einflussfaktoren, Planung, Messung, Management, Munich 2008.

KRÜGER, DIRK/KALBFLEISCH, EBERHARD, Due Diligence bei Kauf und Verkauf von Unternehmen – Rechtliche und steuerliche Aspekte der Vorprüfung beim Unternehmenskauf -, in: DStR, 1999, pp. 174–180.

LANFERMANN, GEORG, Zur Zulässigkeit von Nicht-Prüfungsleistungen nach der EU-Abschlussprüferverordnung, in: BB, 2014, pp. 1771–1775.

LAWSKY, SARAH B., Probably? Understanding tax law's uncertainty, in: University of Pennsylvania Law Review, 2009, Vol. 157, pp. 1017–1074.

LÖFFLER, CHRISTOPH, Tax Due Diligence beim Unternehmenskauf, in: WPg, 2004, pp. 576–583.

LOITZ, RÜDIGER, Audit of Tax – neue Herausforderungen für die integrierte Prüfung der Steuerposten bei einer Abschlussprüfung, in: WPg, 2012, pp. 247–257.

LOITZ, RÜDIGER, Tax Accounting nach ED/2009/2 – ein neuer Standard für die Abbildung von Ertragsteuern in der Finanzberichterstattung, in: DStR, 2009, pp. 2267–2273.

LOITZ, RÜDIGER, Transparente Steuerrisiken durch IFRIC 23, in: DB, 2017, pp. M4–M5.

LÜDENBACH, NORBERT/HOFFMANN, WOLF-DIETER/FREIBERG, JENS, Sec. 26, Steuern vom Einkommen, in: Haufe IFRS Kommentar, published by Lüdenbach, Norbert/Hoffmann, Wolf-Dieter/Freiberg, Jens, 18th edition, Freiburg 2020.

LUDENIA, SASCHA, Analyse entscheidungsrelevanter Risiken im Besteuerungsprozess, Ursachen und Erscheinungsformen steuerlicher Risiken und betriebswirtschaftliche Ansätze zu ihrer Verminderung, Hamburg 2006.

MAMMEN, ANDREAS, Die Berücksichtigung von Ertragsteuerrisiken im Rahmen der Konzernsteuerplanung, in: BFuP, 2011, pp. 502–523.

MEYER, MARCO, Mehr Rechtssicherheit durch den neuen Interpretationsentwurf des IFRS IC zur Abbildung von Betriebsprüfungsrisiken?, in: BB, 2015, pp. 2923–2927.

MEYER, MARCO, Neue Leitlinien zur Abbildung von Betriebsprüfungsrisiken gemäß IFRIC 23 – Update zu BB 2015, 2923 ff., in: BB, 2017, pp. 1771–1774.

MEYER, MARCO, Tax Accounting, in: Tax Compliance: Prävention – Investigation – Remediation – Unternehmensverteidigung, published by Rübenstahl, Markus/Idler, Jesco, Heidelberg 2018, pp. 863–886.

NEUMANN, STEFFEN, Sec. 15 KStG, Ermittlung des Einkommens bei Organschaft, in: Körperschaftsteuergesetz Kommentar, published by Gosch, Dietmar, 4th edition, Munich 2020.

OECD, International Compliance Assurance Programme: Handbook for tax administrations and MNE groups, 2021, available at: https://www.oecd.org/tax/forum-on-tax-administration/publications-and-products/international-compliance-assurance-programme-handbook-for-tax-administrations-and-mne-groups.pdf, accessed on February 13, 2021 at 11:45 a.m.

OECD, Model Tax Convention on Income and on Capital. Condensed Version 2017, Paris 2017.

ONG, AUDRA, The Failure of International Accounting Standards Convergence: A Brief History, in: Review of Integrative Business and Economics Research, 2018, Vol. 7, No. 3, pp. 93–105.

PENATZER, MARKUS, Bilanzierung steuerlicher Risiken nach der Veröffentlichung von IFRIC 23: Unterschiede zum HGB und zu US-GAAP sowie praktische Bedeutung, in: DB, 2018, pp. 777–781.

PILHOFER, JOCHEN/SUERMANN, HENDRIK/MÜLLER, RONJA, Erfassung von Steuerlatenzen im Organkreis nach IFRS – Reflexion ausgewählter praxisrelevanter Fragestellungen, in: PiR, 2014, pp. 159–167.

PRINZ, ULRICH, Bilanzsteuerrecht: Praxisorientierte Bestandsaufnahme aktueller Trends, in: DB, 2021, pp. 9–16.

PRINZ, ULRICH/LUDWIG, FABIAN, ICAP-Pilotprojekt der OECD – Ein neuer internationaler Betriebsprüfungsansatz, in: DB, 2018, pp. 477–478.

PwC, Betriebsprüfung 2018 – Studie zur Praxis der Betriebsprüfung in Deutschland, 2019, available at: https://www.pwc.de/de/steuerberatung/pwc-studie-betriebspruefung-20191.pdf, accessed on February 5, 2021 at 9:45 a.m.

RABY, WILLIAM L./RABY, BURGESS J.W., Quantifying Uncertain Tax Positions, in: Tax Practice, 2006, pp. 1–5.

RISSE, ROBERT, Steuerliches Risikomanagement, in: Ubg, 2012, pp. 169–176.

RISSE, ROBERT, Tax Compliance in der Form der zeitnahen steuerlichen Außenprüfung, in: DB, 2011, pp. 667–674.

ROSE, GERD, Ein Grundgerüst planungsrelevanter Steuerrechtsrisiken, in: Unternehmenstheorie und Besteuerung – Festschrift zum 60. Geburtstag von Dieter Schneider, published by Elschen, Dieter/Schneider, Dieter, Wiesbaden 1995, pp. 479–493.

ROSE, GERD, Steuerberatung und Wissenschaft – Gedanken anläßlich des 50jährigen Bestehens der Betriebswirtschaftlichen Steuerlehre, in: Steuerberater-Jahrbuch 1969/70, published by Gerhard, Thoma/Zacharias, O. H./Niemann, Ursula, Cologne 1970, pp. 31–70.

RUBERG, LARS, IFRIC 23: Berücksichtigung von Unsicherheiten bei der Bilanzierung von Ertragsteuern, in: PiR, 2017, pp. 247–254.

RUBERG, LARS, Neues zur Bilanzierung von Steuerrisiken nach IAS 12, in: PiR, 2016, pp. 10–17.

SCHÄUBLE, JONAS/LACHMANN, MAIK/BASTINI, KAROLA/GETZIN, FARES, Bilanzierung von bestrittenen Steuerschulden nach IFRS und HGB – Ein Überblick vor dem Hintergrund der neuen Regelungen, in: IRZ, 2018, pp. 431–436.

SCHLAGER, JOSEF, Einfluß der Steuerrechtsprognose auf die Risikopolitik der Unternehmung, in: Betriebswirtschaftslehre und Recht: Bericht von der wissenschaftlichen Tagung des Verbandes der Hochschullehrer für Betriebswirtschaft e. V. vom 17. bis 19. Mai 1978 in Nürnberg, published by Heigl, Anton/Uecker, Peter, Wiesbaden 1979, pp. 329–378.

SCHÖN, WOLFGANG, Finanzbeamte auf den Finanzmarkt!?, in: ZHR, 2007, pp. 485–489.

SCHRAMM, HANS-GERHARD, Steuerliche Ungewißheitsanalyse, Grundlagen, Konzept und Expertensystem, Bergisch Gladbach 1989.

SCHULZ-DANSO, MARTIN, Sec. 25, Laufende und latente Ertragsteuern, in: Beck'sches IFRS-Handbuch, published by Brune, Jens/Driesch, Dirk/Schulz-Danso, Martin/Senger, Thomas, 6th edition, Munich 2020.

SEC, Acceptance From Foreign Private Issuers of Financial Statements Prepared in Accordance With International Financial Reporting Standards Without Reconciliation to U.S. GAAP, 2007, available at: https://www.sec.gov/rules/final/2007/33–8879.pdf, accessed on October 15, 2020 at 10:00 a.m.

SELLNER, MARK A., An Early Implementation Guide to Accounting for Uncertain Tax Positions, in: The Tax Executive, 2006, Vol. 58, No. 2, pp. 114–120.

SENGER, THOMAS/DIERSCH, JENS, Sec. 35, Vollkonsolidierung, in: Beck'sches IFRS-Handbuch, published by Brune, Jens/Driesch, Dirk/Schulz-Danso, Martin/Senger, Thomas, 6th edition, Munich 2020.

SHARMA, HIRA/EBERLE, JIM, Rising to the FIN 48 challenge, in: International Tax Review, 2007, Vol. 18, No. 1, pp. 32–34.

SIEGEL, JACK B., Applying FIN 48 to Tax-Exempt Organizations: Too Much of Nothing or It's All Too Much?, in: Tax Notes Today Federal, 2007, pp. 1–38.

SILLIMAN, BENJAMIN R./FITZSIMONS, ADRIAN P., FASB Amends FIN-48: Measurement, Reporting and Disclosure of Income Tax Positions in Financial Reporting, in: Commercial Lending Review, 2007, Vol. 22, No. 6, pp. 38–43.

SIMLACHER, ALFRED, Die Behandlung von unsicheren Ertragsteuerschulden und -forderungen im IFRS-Abschluss: Die Vorschläge des DI/2015/1, in: DB, 2015, pp. 2829–2834.

STÜMPER, FRANZ-PETER/WALTER, WOLFGANG, Erfordernis von Steuerklauseln in Anteilskauf- und anderen Übertragungsverträgen, in: GmbHR, 2008, pp. 31–37.

SUERMANN, HENDRIK/KÄMPFER, NILS/MÜLLER, RONJA, Neuerungen zur Bilanzierung von Ertragsteuern nach IAS 12, in: IRZ, 2016, pp. 413–418.

TREASURE, KATHERINE, Fin 48: Uncertain Tax Positions Associated With Transfer Pricing, 2007, available at: https://www.mondaq.com/unitedstates/tax-authorities/51562/fin-48-uncertain-tax-positions-associated-with-transfer-pricing, accessed on October 15, 2020 at 10:00 a.m.

VÖLK, JULIA/KOBIELLA, CHARLOTTE, ICAP 2.0 – das International Compliance Assurance Programme der OECD, in: IWB, 2019, pp. 637–639.

WACKER, WILHELM, Erfassung und Minimierung steuerlicher Risiken, in: Jahrbuch für Betriebswirte 1981 – Aktuelle Informationen für Wirtschaftspraktiker, published by Kresse, Werner/Alt, Walter, Stuttgart 1981, pp. 259–265.

WALZ, MATTHIAS/BRIESE, JENS/HAAS, MARTIN, IAS 12 – Ertragsteuern, Weinheim 2013.

WARSÖNKE, ANNETTE, Besteuerungsverfahren I – Feststellungs- und Festsetzungsverfahren, 4th edition, Hagen 2020.

WINNEFELD, ROBERT, Sec. J, Handelsrechtlicher Anhang sowie Anhang in der IAS/IFRS-Rechnungslegung, in: Bilanz-Handbuch, published by Winnefeld, Robert, 5th edition, Munich 2015.

WÜNNEMANN, MONIKA, Gesetzlicher Regelungsbedarf für eine zeitnahe Betriebsprüfung, in: Ubg, 2011, pp. 197–203.

ZION, DAVID/VARSHNEY, AMIT, Peeking behind the tax curtain: FIN 48 reveals tax risk, in: Credit Suisse, 2007, pp. 1–18.

ZWIRNER, CHRISTIAN/BUSCH, JULIA, Aktuelle Praxisfragen des IAS 12 – Berücksichtigung von Unsicherheiten bei der Bilanzierung von Ertragsteuern, in: IRZ, 2016, pp. 104–106.

Empirical References

ABERNATHY, JOHN L./BEYER, BROOKE/GROSS, ANDREW D./RAPLEY, ERIC T., Income Statement Reporting Discretion Allowed by FIN 48: Interest and Penalty Expense Classification, in: The Journal of the American Taxation Association, 2017, Vol. 39, No. 1, pp. 45–46.

ALEXANDER, RAQUEL/ETTREDGE, MIKE/STONE, MARY/SUN, LILI, Are mandatory disclosure decisions made strategically? The case of SAB 74 estimates preceding adoption of FIN 48, in: Research in Accounting Regulation, 2011, Vol. 23, No. 2, pp. 160–166.

ALEXANDER, RAQUEL/ETTREDGE, MIKE/STONE, MARY/SUN, LILI, Assessing Uncertain Tax Benefit Aggressiveness, Working Paper, 2009, pp. 1–52, available at: https://papers.ssrn.com/sol3/Delivery.cfm/SSRN_ID1487712_code107148.pdf?abstractid=1085307&mirid=1, accessed on November 16, 2020 at 8:30 a.m.

ALEXANDER, RAQUEL/GROSS, ANDREW/HUSTON, G. RYAN/RICHARDSON, VERNON J., Market Response to FIN 48 Adoption: A Debt Covenant Theory, in: Advances in Taxation, 2017, Vol. 24, pp. 1–36.

ATWOOD, T. J./CAO, YING/DRAKE, MICHAEL S./MYERS, LINDA A., The Usefulness of Income Tax Disclosures Under IFRS versus U.S. GAAP for Predicting Changes in Future Earnings and Cash Flows, Working Paper, 2012, pp. 1–44, available at: https://papers.ssrn.com/sol3/Delivery.cfm/SSRN_ID2181069_code162528.pdf?abstractid=2181069&mirid=1, accessed on November 16, 2020 at 8:30 a.m.

BECK, PAUL J./LISOWSKY, PETRO, Tax Uncertainty and Voluntary Real-Time Tax Audits, in: The Accounting Review, 2014, Vol. 89, No. 3, pp. 867–901.

BLAUFUS, KAY/BOB, JONATHAN/TRINKS, MATTHIAS, How will the court decide? Tax experts and the estimation of tax risk, Working Paper, 2013, pp. 1–24, available at: https://www.econstor.eu/bitstream/10419/88160/1/772793603.pdf, accessed on February 5, 2021 at 5:00 p.m.

BLOUIN, JENNIFER/GLEASON, CRISTI/MILLS, LILLIAN/SIKES, STEPHANIE, Changes in Tax Reserves in Anticipation of FIN 48, Working Paper, 2008, pp. 1–46, available at: https://www8.gsb.columbia.edu/faculty-research/sites/faculty-research/files/accounting/LILMILLS.pdf, accessed on November 16, 2020 at 8:30 a.m.

BLOUIN, JENNIFER/GLEASON, CRISTI/MILLS, LILLIAN/SIKES, STEPHANIE, Pre-Empting Disclosure? Firms' Decisions Prior to FIN No. 48, in: The Accounting Review, 2010, Vol. 85, No. 3, pp. 791–815.

BLOUIN, JENNIFER/GLEASON, CRISTI/MILLS, LILLIAN/SIKES, STEPHANIE, What Can We Learn about Uncertain Tax Benefits from FIN 48?, in: National Tax Journal, 2007, Vol. 60, No. 3, pp. 521–535.

BLOUIN, JENNIFER/ROBINSON, LESLIE, Insights from Academic Participation in the FAF's Initial PIR: The PIR of FIN 48, in: Accounting Horizons, 2014, Vol. 28, No. 3, pp. 479–500.

BLOUIN, JENNIFER/TUNA, İREM, Tax Contingencies: Cushioning the blow to earnings?, Working Paper, 2007, pp. 1–48, available at: https://users.nber.org/~confer/2006/frtf06/blouin.pdf, accessed on November 16, 2020 at 8:30 a.m.

BORKOWSKI, SUSAN C./GAFFNEY, MARY ANNE, FIN 48, uncertainty and transfer pricing: (Im)Perfect together?, in: Journal of International Accounting, Auditing and Taxation, 2012, Vol. 21, No. 1, pp. 32–51.

BORKOWSKI, SUSAN C./GAFFNEY, MARY ANNE, Proactive Transfer Pricing Risk Management in PATA Countries, in: Journal of International Accounting Research, 2014, Vol. 13, No. 2, pp. 25–55.

BOZANIC, ZAHN/HOOPES, JEFFREY L./THORNOCK, JACOB R./WILLIAMS, BRADEN M., IRS Attention, in: Journal of Accounting Research, 2017, Vol. 55, No. 1, pp. 79–114.

BROWN, JENNIFER L./DRAKE, KATHARINE D./MARTIN, MELISSA A., Compensation in the Post-FIN 48 Period: The Case of Contracting on Tax Performance and Uncertainty, in: Contemporary Accounting Research, 2016, Vol. 33, No. 1, pp. 121–151.

CAZIER, RICHARD/REGO, SONJA/TIAN, XIAOLI/WILSON, RYAN, Did FIN 48 Limit the Use of Tax Reserves as a Tool for Earnings Management?, Working Paper, 2011, pp. 1–47, available at: https://papers.ssrn.com/sol3/Delivery.cfm/SSRN_ID1910815_code281414.pdf?abstractid=1656012&mirid=1, accessed on November 16, 2020 at 8:30 a.m.

CAZIER, RICHARD/REGO, SONJA/TIAN, XIAOLI/WILSON, RYAN, Early Evidence on the Determinants of Unrecognized Tax Benefits, Working Paper, 2009, pp. 1–40, available at: https://papers.ssrn.com/sol3/Delivery.cfm/SSRN_ID1578485_code281414.pdf?abstractid=1578485&mirid=1, accessed on November 16, 2020 at 8:30 a.m.

CAZIER, RICHARD/REGO, SONJA/TIAN, XIAOLI/WILSON, RYAN, The impact of increased disclosure requirements and the standardization of accounting practices on earnings management through the reserve for income taxes, in: Review of Accounting Studies, 2015, Vol. 20, No. 1, pp. 436–469.

CHUNG, SUNG GON/GOH, BENG WEE/LEE, JIMMY/SHEVLIN, TERRY, Corporate Tax Aggressiveness and Insider Trading, in: Contemporary Accounting Research, 2019, Vol. 36, No. 1, pp. 230–258.

CICONTE, WILLIAM A./DONOHOE, MICHAEL P./LISOWSKY, PETRO/MAYBERRY, MICHAEL A., Predictable Uncertainty: The Relation Between Unrecognized Tax Benefits and Future Income Tax Cash Outflows, Working Paper, 2016, pp. 1–53, available at: https://papers.ssrn.com/sol3/Delivery.cfm/SSRN_ID2846069_code831551.pdf?abstractid=2390150&mirid=1, accessed on November 16, 2020 at 8:30 a.m.

DAVIS, ANN BOYD, The Impact of FIN 48 and Economic Nexus on Multistate Tax Settlements, Working Paper, 2011, pp. 1–41, available at: https://papers.ssrn.com/sol3/Delivery.cfm/SSRN_ID1905025_code1697687.pdf?abstractid=1905025&mirid=1, accessed on November 16, 2020 at 8:30 a.m.

DE SIMONE, LISA/NICKERSON, JORDAN/SEIDMAN, JERI/STOMBERG, BRIDGET, How Reliably Do Empirical Tests Identify Tax Avoidance?, in: Contemporary Accounting Research, 2020, Vol. 37, No. 3, pp. 1536–1561.

DE SIMONE, LISA/ROBINSON, JOHN R./STOMBERG, BRIDGET, Distilling the reserve for uncertain tax positions: the revealing case of black liquor, in: Review of Accounting Studies, 2014, Vol. 19, No. 1, pp. 456–472.

DE WAEGENAERE, ANJA/SANSING, RICHARD/WIELHOUWER, JACCO L., Financial accounting measures of tax reporting aggressiveness, Working Paper, 2010, pp. 1–30, available at: https://papers.ssrn.com/sol3/Delivery.cfm/SSRN_ID2251881_code16942.pdf?abstractid=1697536&mirid=1, accessed on November 16, 2020 at 8:30 a.m.

DRAKE, KATHARINE D./LUSCH, STEPHEN J./STEKELBERG, JAMES, Does Tax Risk Affect Investor Valuation of Tax Avoidance?, in: Journal of Accounting, Auditing & Finance, 2019, Vol. 34, No. 1, pp. 151–176.

DUNBAR, AMY/KOLBASOVSKY, LINDA/PHILLIPS, JOHN, FIN 48 Adoption Disclosures, Working Paper, 2007, pp. 1–19, available at: https://papers.ssrn.com/sol3/Delivery.cfm/SSRN_ID1023906_code22420.pdf?abstractid=1023906&mirid=1, accessed on November 16, 2020 at 8:30 a.m.

DUNBAR, AMY/OMER, THOMAS C./SCHULTZ, THOMAS D., The Informativeness of FIN 48 "Look-Forward" Disclosures, Working Paper, 2010, pp. 1–44, available at: https://papers.ssrn.com/sol3/Delivery.cfm/SSRN_ID1633626_code22420.pdf?abstractid=1633626&mirid=1, accessed on November 16, 2020 at 8:30 a.m.

ERICKSON, MATTHEW J./GOLDMAN, NATHAN C./STEKELBERG, JAMES, The Cost of Compliance: FIN 48 and Audit Fees, in: The Journal of the American Taxation Association, 2016, Vol. 38, No. 2, pp. 67–85.

FAF, Accounting for Uncertainty in Income Taxes. Post-Implementation Review Report on FASB Interpretation No. 48., 2012, available at: https://www.accountingfoundation.org/cs/BlobServer?blobkey=id&blobnocache=true&blobwhere=1175832847294&blobheader=application%2Fpdf&blobheadername2=Content-Length&blobheadername1=Content-Disposition&blobheadervalue2=518417b&blobheadervalue1=filename%3DPIR_Report_FIN_48.pdf&blobcol=urldata&blobtable=MungoBlobs, accessed on October 20, 2021 at 08:15 a.m.

FINLEY, ANDREW R., The impact of large tax settlement favorability on firms' subsequent tax avoidance, in: Review of Accounting Studies, 2019, Vol. 24, No. 1, pp. 156–187.

FLEISCHMAN, GARY/WEST, ASHLEY NICOLE, The Role of Trait and State Moral Disengagement on FIN 48 Earnings Management, Working Paper, 2019, pp. 1–47, available at: https://papers.ssrn.com/sol3/Delivery.cfm/SSRN_ID3545345_code2441830.pdf?abstractid=3248378&mirid=1, accessed on November 16, 2020 at 8:30 a.m.

FRISCHMANN, PETER J./SHEVLIN, TERRY/WILSON, RYAN, Economic consequences of increasing the conformity in accounting for uncertain tax benefits, in: Journal of Accounting and Economics, 2008, Vol. 46, No. 2–3, pp. 261–278.

FURNER, ZHAN Z., Assessment of FIN 48 liabilities: A proposed experiment highlighting flexible uncertainty, in: Southwestern Economic Review, 2017, Vol. 44, pp. 75–98.

GLEASON, CRISTI A./MARKLE, KEVIN S./SONG, JANE Z., Did FIN 48 improve the predictive ability of tax expense? Evidence from a comparison with IFRS firms, Working Paper, 2018, pp. 1–41, available at: https://krannert.purdue.edu/academics/Accounting/bkd_speakers/papers/GMS.pdf, accessed on November 16, 2020 at 8:30 a.m.

GLEASON, CRISTI A./MILLS, LILLIAN F./NESSA, MICHELLE L., Does FIN 48 Improve Firms' Estimates of Tax Reserves?, in: Contemporary Accounting Research, 2018, Vol. 35, No. 3, pp. 1395–1429.

GOLDMAN, NATHAN/LAMPENIUS, NIKLAS/RADHAKRISHNAN, SURESH/STENZEL, ARTHUR/FERES DE ALMEIDA, JOSE ELIAS, FASB Interpretation Number 48 (FIN 48) Disclosures and Corporate Innovation, Working Paper, 2020, pp. 1–52, available at: https://papers.ssrn.com/sol3/Delivery.cfm/SSRN_ID3724592_code1898808.pdf?abstractid=3174891&mirid=1, accessed on November 16, 2020 at 8:30 a.m.

GROSS, ANDREW D., Does Mandatory Disclosure Affect Recognition of Contingent Liabilities? Evidence from FIN 48, Working Paper, 2011, pp. 1–41, available at: https://papers.ssrn.com/sol3/Delivery.cfm/SSRN_ID1905207_code1697687.pdf?abstractid=1905207&mirid=1, accessed on November 16, 2020 at 8:30 a.m.

GUENTHER, DAVID A./WILSON, RYAN J./WU, KAISHU, Tax Uncertainty and Incremental Tax Avoidance, in: The Accounting Review, 2019, Vol. 94, No. 2, pp. 229–247.

GUPTA, SANJAY/LAUX, RICK C./LYNCH, DANIEL P., Do Firms Use Tax Reserves to Meet Analysts' Forecasts? Evidence from the Pre- and Post-FIN 48 Periods, in: Contemporary Accounting Research, 2016, Vol. 33, No. 3, pp. 1044–1074.

GUPTA, SANJAY/MILLS, LILLIAN F./TOWERY, ERIN M., The Effect of Mandatory Financial Statement Disclosures of Tax Uncertainty on Tax Reporting and Collections: The Case of FIN 48 and Multistate Tax Avoidance, in: The Journal of the American Taxation Association, 2014, Vol. 36, No. 2, pp. 203–229.

HANLON, MICHELLE/MAYDEW, EDWARD L./SAAVEDRA, DANIEL, The taxman cometh: Does tax uncertainty affect corporate cash holdings?, in: Review of Accounting Studies, 2017, Vol. 22, No. 3, pp. 1198–1228.

HASAN, IFTEKHAR/HOI, CHUN KEUNG/WU, QIANG/ZHANG, HAO, Beauty is in the eye of the beholder: The effect of corporate tax avoidance on the cost of bank loans, in: Journal of Financial Economics, 2014, Vol. 113, No. 1, pp. 109–130.

HENRY, ERIN/MASSEL, NORMAN/TOWERY, ERIN, Increased tax disclosures and corporate tax avoidance, in: National Tax Journal, 2016, Vol. 69, No. 4, pp. 809–830.

HOGAN, BRIAN/NOGA, TRACY, Auditor-provided tax services and long-term tax avoidance, in: Review of Accounting and Finance, 2015, Vol. 14, No. 3, pp. 285–305.

HOI, CHUN KEUNG/WU, QIANG/ZHANG, HAO, Is Corporate Social Responsibility (CSR) Associated with Tax Avoidance? Evidence from Irresponsible CSR Activities, in: The Accounting Review, 2013, Vol. 88, No. 6, pp. 2025–2059.

JACOB, MARTIN/WENTLAND, KELLY/WENTLAND, SCOTT, Real Effects of Tax Uncertainty: Evidence from Firm Capital Investments, Working Paper, 2020, pp. 1–21, available at: https://papers.ssrn.com/sol3/Delivery.cfm/SSRN_ID3695044_code1563689.pdf?abstractid=2518243&mirid=1, accessed on November 16, 2020 at 8:30 a.m.

KLASSEN, KENNETH J./LISOWSKY, PETRO/MESCALL, DEVAN, The Role of Auditors, Non-Auditors, and Internal Tax Departments in Corporate Tax Aggressiveness, in: The Accounting Review, 2016, Vol. 91, No. 1, pp. 179–205.

KLASSEN, KENNETH J./LISOWSKY, PETRO/MESCALL, DEVAN, Transfer Pricing: Strategies, Practices, and Tax Minimization, in: Contemporary Accounting Research, 2017, Vol. 34, No. 1, pp. 455–493.

KOESTER, ALLISON, Investor Valuation of Tax Avoidance Through Uncertain Tax Positions, Working Paper, 2011, pp. 1–50, available at: https://papers.ssrn.com/sol3/Delivery.cfm/SSRN_ID1905210_code1697687.pdf?abstractid=1905210&mirid=1, accessed on November 16, 2020 at 8:30 a.m.

LEE, NAMRYOUNG/SWENSON, CHARLES, Shock and Law: Fin 48 Report Card, IFRS, and Beyond, in: International Journal of Economics and Finance, 2010, Vol. 2, No. 3, pp. 222–233.

LISOWSKY, PETRO, Seeking Shelter: Empirically Modeling Tax Shelters Using Financial Statement Information, in: The Accounting Review, 2010, Vol. 85, No. 5, pp. 1693–1720.

LISOWSKY, PETRO/ROBINSON, LESLIE A./SCHMIDT, ANDREW, An Examination of FIN 48: Tax Shelters, Auditor Independence, and Corporate Governance, Working Paper, 2009, pp. 1–49, available at: https://www0.gsb.columbia.edu/mygsb/faculty/research/pubfiles/3722/schmidt_FIN48.pdf, accessed on November 16, 2020 at 8:30 a.m.

LISOWSKY, PETRO/ROBINSON, LESLIE A./SCHMIDT, ANDREW, Do Publicly Disclosed Tax Reserves Tell Us About Privately Disclosed Tax Shelter Activity?, in: Journal of Accounting Research, 2013, Vol. 51, No. 3, pp. 583–629.

MILLS, LILLIAN F./ROBINSON, LESLIE A./SANSING, RICHARD C., FIN 48 and Tax Compliance, in: The Accounting Review, 2010, Vol. 85, No. 5, pp. 1721–1742.

NICHOLS, NANCY B., One Year Later: An Analysis of FIN 48 Disclosures in 2007 Forms 10-K, in: Tax Notes, 2008, pp. 555–562.

NICHOLS, NANCY B./BRIGGS, JOHN W./BARIL, CHARLES P., And the Impact Is . . . First-Quarter Results From Adopting FIN 48, in: Tax Notes, 2007, pp. 377–388.

NICHOLS, NANCY B./BRIGGS, JOHN W./BARIL, CHARLES P., Early Indications of the Impact of FIN 48, in: Tax Notes, 2007, pp. 215–226.

ROBINSON, LESLIE A./SAVOR, PAVEL/SIKES, STEPHANIE, Value Relevance of Income Tax Expense Post FIN 48, Working Paper, 2017, pp. 1–35, available at: https://faculty.wharton.upenn.edu/wp-content/uploads/2017/04/RSS-20170409.pdf, accessed on November 16, 2020 at 8:30 a.m.

ROBINSON, LESLIE A./SCHMIDT, ANDREW P., Firm and Investor Responses to Uncertain Tax Benefit Disclosure Requirements, in: The Journal of the American Taxation Association, 2013, Vol. 35, No. 2, pp. 85–120.

ROBINSON, LESLIE A./STOMBERG, BRIDGET/TOWERY, ERIN M., One Size Does Not Fit All: How the Uniform Rules of FIN 48 Affect the Relevance of Income Tax Accounting, in: The Accounting Review, 2016, Vol. 91, No. 4, pp. 1195–1217.

SONG, WEI-LING/TUCKER, ALAN L., Corporate Tax Reserves, Firm Value, and Leverage, Working Paper, 2008, pp. 1–33, available at: https://papers.ssrn.com/sol3/Delivery.cfm/SSRN_ID1086827_code272206.pdf?abstractid=1086827&mirid=1, accessed on November 16, 2020 at 8:30 a.m.

TAYLOR, GRANTLEY/RICHARDSON, GRANT/AL-HADI, AHMED, Uncertain tax benefits, international tax risk, and audit specialization: Evidence from US multinational firms, in: International Journal of Auditing, 2018, Vol. 22, No. 2, pp. 230–248.

TOMOHARA, AKINORI/LEE, JIM/LEE, SEUNGRAE, Did FIN 48 increase companies' tax payments? Trade-off between disclosure and tax burdens, in: Applied Economics, 2012, Vol. 44, No. 32, pp. 4239–4248.

WATRIN, CHRISTOPH/BURGGRAEF, STEPHAN/WEISS, FALKO, Auditor-Provided Tax Services and Accounting for Tax Uncertainty, in: The International Journal of Accounting, 2019, Vol. 54, No. 3, pp. 1950011-1-1950011-52.

List of Comment Letters

ACCA, Comment Letter No. 22 to IFRIC 23, 2016, available at: http://eifrs.ifrs.org/eifrs/comment_letters//63/63_6242_YenpeiChenACCA_0_IFRICInterpretationDI20151UTPconsultationresponse_final.pdf, accessed on November 23, 2020 at 2:00 p.m.

ACSEC, Comment Letter No. 17 to FIN 48, 2005, available at: https://www.fasb.org/document/blob?fileName=33808.pdf, accessed on November 23, 2020 at 4:30 p.m.

BB&T, Comment Letter No. 8 to FIN 48, 2005, available at: https://www.fasb.org/document/blob?fileName=33765.pdf, accessed on November 23, 2020 at 4:30 p.m.

BDO, Comment Letter No. 59 to IFRIC 23, 2016, available at: http://eifrs.ifrs.org/eifrs/comment_letters//63/63_6355_AndrewBuchananBDO_0_BDOCLDI201501.pdf, accessed on November 23, 2020 at 2:00 p.m.

BDO, Comment Letter No. 80 to FIN 48, 2005, available at: https://www.fasb.org/document/blob?fileName=34385.pdf, accessed on November 23, 2020 at 4:30 p.m.

BUSINESS EUROPE, Comment Letter No. 35 to IFRIC 23, 2016, available at: http://eifrs.ifrs.org/eifrs/comment_letters//63/63_6267_ErikBerggrenBUSINESSEUROPE_0_L0119_UncertaintyoverIncomeTaxTreatment.pdf, accessed on November 23, 2020 at 2:00 p.m.

DELOITTE, Comment Letter No. 108 to FIN 48, 2005, available at: https://www.fasb.org/document/blob?fileName=34614.pdf, accessed on November 23, 2020 at 4:30 p.m.

DELOITTE, Comment Letter No. 32 to IFRIC 23, 2016, available at: http://eifrs.ifrs.org/eifrs/comment_letters//63/63_6263_VeronicaPooleDeloitteToucheTohmatsuLimited_0_DTTLCommentLetterDI20151UncertaintyoverIncomeTaxTreatments.pdf, accessed on November 23, 2020 at 2:00 p.m.

DRSC, Comment Letter No. 12 to IFRIC 23, 2016, available at: http://eifrs.ifrs.org/eifrs/comment_letters//63/63_6211_AndreasBarckowASCG_0_160114_CL_ASCG_IFRSIC_IFRIC_DI_IAS12.pdf, accessed on November 23, 2020 at 2:00 p.m.

EFRAG, Comment Letter No. 60 to IFRIC 23, 2016, available at: http://eifrs.ifrs.org/eifrs/comment_letters//63/63_6469_MartinSvitekEFRAG_0_EFRAG__CommentLetter__UncertaintyoverIncomeTaxTreatments.pdf, accessed on November 23, 2020 at 2:00 p.m.

ESMA, Comment Letter No. 18 to IFRIC 23, 2016, available at: http://eifrs.ifrs.org/eifrs/comment_letters//63/63_6228_StevenMaijoorESMA_0_2016ESMA35ESMACLtotheIFRSICDIUncertaintaxpositions.pdf, accessed on November 23, 2020 at 2:00 p.m.

EY, Comment Letter No. 107 to FIN 48, 2005, available at: https://www.fasb.org/document/blob?fileName=34598.pdf, accessed on November 23, 2020 at 4:30 p.m.

EY, Comment Letter No. 16 to IFRIC 23, 2016, available at: http://eifrs.ifrs.org/eifrs/comment_letters//63/63_6225_VictoriaOLearyErnstYoung_0_EYcommentletterDraftIFRICInterpretationUncertaintyoverIncomeTaxTreatments.pdf, accessed on November 23, 2020 at 2:00 p.m.

FASB, Summary of Comment Letters to FIN 48, 2005, available at: https://www.fasb.org/project/utp_cl_summary.pdf, accessed on October 17, 2020 at 5:00 p.m.

FEI, Comment Letter No. 20 to FIN 48, 2005, available at: https://www.fasb.org/document/blob?fileName=33862.pdf, accessed on November 23, 2020 at 4:30 p.m.

GRANT THORNTON, Comment Letter No. 9 to IFRIC 23, 2016, available at: http://eifrs.ifrs.org/eifrs/comment_letters//63/63_6189_AndrewWatchmanGrantThorntonInternational_0_CommentletterDI20151UncertaintyoverIncomeTaxTreatmentsJan2016FINAL.pdf, accessed on November 23, 2020 at 2:00 p.m.

GROVE TAX POLICY INSTITUTE, Comment Letter No. 47 to IFRIC 23, 2016, available at: http://eifrs.ifrs.org/eifrs/comment_letters//63/63_6294_VernorSoghughGroveTaxPolicy_0_IFRICUncertainTaxPositionsCommentLetterJanuary182016VSoghughFinal.pdf, accessed on November 23, 2020 at 2:00 p.m.

HARVEY, RICHARD J., Comment Letter No. 5 to FIN 48, 2005, available at: https://www.fasb.org/document/blob?fileName=33644.pdf, accessed on November 23, 2020 at 4:30 p.m.

IASB, Summary of Comment Letters to IFRIC 23, 2016, available at: https://cdn.ifrs.org/-/media/feature/meetings/2016/july/ifrs-ic/ias-12-income-taxes/ap7-uncertainty-over-income-tax-treatments.pdf, accessed on October 17, 2020 at 5:00 p.m.

KPMG, Comment Letter No. 37 to IFRIC 23, 2016, available at: http://eifrs.ifrs.org/eifrs/comment_letters//63/63_6274_MarkVaeseenKPMGIFRGLimited_0_KPMGcommentletteronDI_2015_1UncertaintyoverIncomeTaxTreatments.pdf, accessed on November 23, 2020 at 2:00 p.m.

KPMG, Comment Letter No. 85 to FIN 48, 2005, available at: https://www.fasb.org/document/blob?fileName=34428.pdf, accessed on November 23, 2020 at 4:30 p.m.

MAZARS, Comment Letter No. 30 to IFRIC 23, 2016, available at: http://eifrs.ifrs.org/eifrs/comment_letters//63/63_6256_BARBETMASSINMICHELMAZARS_0_MazarsCommentLetteronDraftIFRICInterpretationonUncertaintyoverIncomeTaxTreatments.pdf, accessed on November 23, 2020 at 2:00 p.m.

MORGAN STANLEY, Comment Letter No. 109 to FIN 48, 2005, available at: https://www.fasb.org/document/blob?fileName=34713.pdf, accessed on November 23, 2020 at 4:30 p.m.

NESTLE, Comment Letter No. 58 to IFRIC 23, 2016, available at: http://eifrs.ifrs.org/eifrs/comment_letters//63/63_6332_FrancoisAndreoliNestle_0_NestlecommentletterDraftIFRICDI20151.pdf, accessed on November 23, 2020 at 2:00 p.m.

PwC, Comment Letter No. 39 to IFRIC 23, 2016, available at: http://eifrs.ifrs.org/eifrs/comment_letters//63/63_6278_TonyDebellPwC_0_PwCresponseIFRICIntUncertaintyoverIncomeTaxTreatments19Jan2016.pdf, accessed on November 23, 2020 at 2:00 p.m.

PwC, Comment Letter No. 97 to FIN 48, 2005, available at: https://www.fasb.org/document/blob?fileName=34510.pdf, accessed on November 23, 2020 at 4:30 p.m.

SIEMENS, Comment Letter No. 11 to IFRIC 23, 2016, available at: http://eifrs.ifrs.org/eifrs/comment_letters//63/63_6206_JuergenSieberSiemensAG_0_Comment_Letter_Siemens.pdf, accessed on November 23, 2020 at 2:00 p.m.

TEI, Comment Letter No. 45 to FIN 48, 2005, available at: https://www.fasb.org/document/blob?fileName=34183.pdf, accessed on November 23, 2020 at 4:30 p.m.

TELEFONICA, Comment Letter No. 57 to IFRIC 23, 2016, available at: http://eifrs.ifrs.org/eifrs/comment_letters//63/63_6324_MartaSotoTelefnica_0_CommentletterDI2015_1TEF.pdf, accessed on November 23, 2020 at 2:00 p.m.

List of Consolidated Financial Statements

ADIDAS, Annual Report 2019, 2020, available at: https://report.adidas-group.com/2019/en/servicepages/downloads/files/adidas_annual_report_2019.pdf, accessed on January 15, 2021 at 9:15 a.m.

AAREAL BANK, Annual Report 2019, 2020, available at: https://www.aareal-bank.com/fileadmin/downloadlist/DAM_Content/IR/Finanzberichte/2019/191231_gb_en.pdf, accessed on January 15, 2021 at 9:15 a.m.

AIRBUS, Annual Report 2019, 2020, available at: https://annualreport.airbus.com/pdf/Airbus%20Annual%20Report%202019.pdf, accessed on January 15, 2021 at 9:15 a.m.

AIXTRON, Annual Report 2019, 2020, available at: https://www.aixtron.com/investoren/publikationen/2019/en/Annual%20Report%202019.pdf, accessed on January 15, 2021 at 9:15 a.m.

ALLIANZ, Annual Report 2019, 2020, available at: https://www.allianz.com/content/dam/onemarketing/azcom/Allianz_com/investor-relations/en/results-reports/annual-report/ar-2019/en-AR-Group-Annual-Report-Allianz-2019.pdf, accessed on January 15, 2021 at 9:15 a.m.

ALSTRIA, Annual Report 2019, 2020, available at: https://alstria.com/wp-content/uploads/2020/02/Annual_Report_2019.pdf, accessed on January 15, 2021 at 9:15 a.m.

AROUNDTOWN, Annual Report 2019, 2020, available at: https://www.aroundtown.de/fileadmin/user_upload/04_investor_relations/downloads/2019/AT_FY_2019.pdf, accessed on January 15, 2021 at 9:15 a.m.

AURUBIS, Annual Report 2018/2019, 2019, available at: https://www.aurubis.com/binaries/content/assets/aurubisrelaunch/files/finanzberichte-de/2018–19/q4/aurubis_annual-report_fy_18_19_2019_12_11.pdf, accessed on January 15, 2021 at 9:15 a.m.

BASF, Annual Report 2019, 2020, available at: https://report.basf.com/2019/en/servicepages/downloads/files/BASF_Report_2019.pdf, accessed on January 15, 2021 at 9:15 a.m.

BAYER, Annual Report 2019, 2020, available at: https://www.bayer.com/sites/default/files/2020–11/bayer-ag-annual-report-2019_6.pdf, accessed on January 15, 2021 at 9:15 a.m.

BECHTLE, Annual Report 2019, 2020, available at: https://www.bechtle.com/dam/jcr:9eead133–7362–4d8c-a68b-9e5ca7b931c2/bechtle_gb19_en.pdf, accessed on January 15, 2021 at 9:15 a.m.

BEIERSDORF, Annual Report 2019, 2020, available at: https://www.beiersdorf.com/~/media/Beiersdorf/investors/financial-reports/2020/annual-report/Beiersdorf-2019-Annual-Report-en.PDF, accessed on January 15, 2021 at 9:15 a.m.

BMW, Annual Report 2019, 2020, available at: https://www.bmwgroup.com/content/dam/grpw/websites/bmwgroup_com/ir/downloads/en/2020/hauptversammlung/BMW-Group-Annual-Report-2019.pdf, accessed on January 15, 2021 at 9:15 a.m.

BRENNTAG, Annual Report 2019, 2020, available at: https://www.brenntag.com/corporate/media/documents/investor_relations/2020/brenntag_annualreport_2019.pdf, accessed on January 15, 2021 at 9:15 a.m.

CANCOM, Annual Report 2019, 2020, available at: https://www.cancom.de/wp-content/uploads/sites/7/2020/04/200430_CANCOM_AnnualReport2019.pdf, accessed on January 15, 2021 at 9:15 a.m.

CARL ZEISS MEDITEC, Annual Report 2018/2019, 2019, available at: https://applications.zeiss.com/C1257A290053AE30/0/A073B3074386C840C12584C700708953/$FILE/AFX_Annual_Report_2018-19_Long_Version-1.pdf, accessed on January 15, 2021 at 9:30 a.m.

COMMERZBANK, Annual Report 2019, 2020, available at: https://www.commerzbank.de/media/aktionaere/service/archive/konzern/2020_4/Geschaeftsbericht_2019_Konzern_EN.pdf, accessed on January 15, 2021 at 9:30 a.m.

COMPUGROUP MEDICAL, Annual Report 2019, 2020, available at: https://www.cgm.com/_Resources/Persistent/ff4db48e3506b7ac45e867503ee3854c78b4cf5d/25032020_2019_EN_CGM_Geschaeftsbericht.pdf, accessed on January 15, 2021 at 9:30 a.m.

CONTINENTAL, Annual Report 2019, 2020, available at: https://www.continental.com/resource/blob/216556/d579acf1e6ae8f79d3b1cd44bb37f169/annual-report-2019-data.pdf, accessed on January 15, 2021 at 9:30 a.m.

COVESTRO, Annual Report 2019, 2020, available at: https://www.covestro.com/-/media/covestro/country-sites/global/documents/investrors/reports/overview/annual-financial-statements/07_covestro_ag_financial_statements_2019.pdf?la=en, accessed on January 15, 2021 at 9:30 a.m.

CTS EVENTIM, Annual Report 2019, 2020, available at: https://corporate.eventim.de/fileadmin/user_upload/eventim/04_investor_relations/zahlen/finanzberichte/2019/en/AnnualReport_2019.pdf, accessed on January 15, 2021 at 9:30 a.m.

DAIMLER, Annual Report 2019, 2020, available at: https://www.daimler.com/documents/investors/reports/annual-report/daimler/daimler-ir-annual-report-2019-incl-combined-management-report-daimler-ag.pdf, accessed on January 15, 2021 at 9:30 a.m.

DELIVERY HERO, Annual Report 2019, 2020, available at: https://ir.deliveryhero.com/download/companies/delivery/Annual%20Reports/DE000A2E4K43-JA-2019-EQ-E-00.pdf, accessed on January 15, 2021 at 9:30 a.m.

DEUTSCHE BANK, Annual Report 2019, 2020, available at: https://www.db.com/ir/en/download/Deutsche_Bank_Annual_Report_2019.pdf, accessed on January 15, 2021 at 9:30 a.m.

DEUTSCHE BÖRSE, Annual Report 2019, 2020, available at: https://www.deutsche-boerse.com/resource/blob/1749866/27390e8dd169dbfd63f867700d4c816a/data/DBG-annual-report-2019.pdf, accessed on January 15, 2021 at 9:30 a.m.

DEUTSCHE LUFTHANSA, Annual Report 2019, 2020, available at: https://investor-relations.lufthansagroup.com/fileadmin/downloads/en/financial-reports/annual-reports/LH-AR-2019-e.pdf, accessed on January 15, 2021 at 9:30 a.m.

DEUTSCHE POST, Annual Report 2019, 2020, available at: https://www.dpdhl.com/content/dam/dpdhl/en/media-center/investors/documents/annual-reports/DPDHL-2019-Annual-Report.pdf, accessed on January 15, 2021 at 9:30 a.m.

DEUTSCHE TELEKOM, Annual Report 2019, 2020, available at: https://report.telekom.com/annual-report-2019/servicepages/downloads/files/entire_dtag_ar19.pdf, accessed on January 15, 2021 at 9:30 a.m.

DEUTSCHE WOHNEN, Annual Report 2019, 2020, available at: https://ir.deutsche-wohnen.com/download/companies/dewohnen/Annual%20Reports/DW_Annual_Report_2019.pdf, accessed on January 15, 2021 at 9:30 a.m.

DÜRR, Annual Report 2019, 2020, available at: https://www.durr-group.com/fileadmin/durr-group.com/Investors/Downloads/Reports/2019/Annual-Report-2019-EN.pdf, accessed on January 15, 2021 at 9:30 a.m.

E.ON, Annual Report 2019, 2020, available at: https://www.eon.com/content/dam/eon/eon-com/investors/annual-report/GB19_US_final.pdf, accessed on January 15, 2021 at 9:45 a.m.

EVONIK, Annual Report 2019, 2020, available at: https://corporate.evonik.com/Downloads/Corporate/BPK/Evonik_Financial_Report_2019.pdf, accessed on January 15, 2021 at 9:45 a.m.

EVOTEC, Annual Report 2019, 2020, available at: https://www.evotec.com/f/8f443bae31f2f8a01cb2032404962eb6.pdf, accessed on January 15, 2021 at 9:45 a.m.

FRAPORT, Annual Report 2019, 2020, available at: https://www.fraport.com/content/dam/fraport-company/documents/investoren/eng/publications/annual-reports/Annual%20Report%202019.pdf/_jcr_content/renditions/original.media_file.download_attachment.file/Annual%20Report%202019.pdf, accessed on January 15, 2021 at 9:45 a.m.

FREENET, Annual Report 2019, 2020, available at: https://blob.freent.de/contentblob/7725074/3/data/20200327-annual-report.pdf, accessed on January 15, 2021 at 9:45 a.m.

FRESENIUS MEDICAL CARE, Annual Report 2019, 2020, available at: https://www.freseniusmedicalcare.com/fileadmin/data/com/pdf/Media_Center/Publications/Annual_Reports/FME_Annual_Report_2019.pdf, accessed on January 15, 2021 at 9:45 a.m.

FRESENIUS, Annual Report 2019, 2020, available at: https://www.fresenius.com/financial_reporting/Fresenius_Annual_Report_2019.pdf, accessed on January 15, 2021 at 9:45 a.m.

FUCHS PETROLUB, Annual Report 2019, 2020, available at: https://www.fuchs.com/group/the-company/company/download-center/download/file/179731-annual-report-2019/, accessed on January 15, 2021 at 9:45 a.m.

GEA, Annual Report 2019, 2020, available at: https://www.gea.com/en/binaries/gea-annual-report-2019_tcm11-66349.pdf, accessed on January 15, 2021 at 9:45 a.m.

GERRESHEIMER, Annual Report 2019, 2019, available at: https://www.gerresheimer.com/fileadmin/user_upload/user_upload/Company/Investor_Relations/annual-general-meeting/2020/20200219_Gerresheimer_Annual_Report_2019.pdf, accessed on January 15, 2021 at 9:45 a.m.

GRAND CITY PROPERTIES, Annual Report 2019, 2020, available at: https://www.grandcityproperties.com/fileadmin/user_upload/03_investor_relations/Downloads/2019/GCP_FY_2019.pdf, accessed on January 15, 2021 at 9:45 a.m.

HANNOVER RÜCK, Annual Report 2019, 2020, available at: https://www.hannover-re.com/1528650/annual-report-2019.pdf, accessed on January 15, 2021 at 9:45 a.m.

HEIDELBERG CEMENT, Annual Report 2019, 2020, available at: https://www.heidelbergcement.com/en/system/files_force/assets/document/f2/98/annual_report_2019.pdf?download=1, accessed on January 15, 2021 at 9:45 a.m.

HELLA, Annual Report 2018/2019, 2019, available at: https://www.hella.com/hella-com/assets/media_global/2019.08.09_HELLA_Annual_Report_2019_SECURED.pdf, accessed on January 15, 2021 at 9:45 a.m.

HELLOFRESH, Annual Report 2019, 2020, available at: https://ir.hellofreshgroup.com/download/companies/hellofresh/Hauptversammlung/AGM_HF_2020_Annual_Report_2019.pdf, accessed on January 15, 2021 at 9:45 a.m.

HENKEL, Annual Report 2019, 2020, available at: https://www.henkel.com/resource/blob/1038542/08060f027f19e809b0eb3d95cbbc9946/data/2019-annual-report.pdf, accessed on January 15, 2021 at 10:00 a.m.

HOCHTIEF, Annual Report 2019, 2020, available at: https://www.hochtief.de/mmdbdownload?id=187999&format=4, accessed on January 15, 2021 at 10:00 a.m.

HUGO BOSS, Annual Report 2019, 2020, available at: https://group.hugoboss.com/fileadmin/media/pdf/sustainability/sustainability_reports_EN/HUGO_BOSS_Annual_Report_2019.pdf, accessed on January 15, 2021 at 10:00 a.m.

INFINEON, Annual Report 2019, 2019, available at: https://www.infineon.com/dgdl/Infineon+Annual+Report+2019.pdf?fileId=5546d4616e8d476e016e9958480f0029, accessed on January 15, 2021 at 10:00 a.m.

K+S, Annual Report 2019, 2020, available at: https://www.kpluss.com/en-us/.pdf/investor-relations/2020/2020-annual-general-meeting/annual-report-2019.pdf, accessed on January 15, 2021 at 10:00 a.m.

KION GROUP, Annual Report 2019, 2020, available at: https://reports.kiongroup.com/2019/ar/servicepages/downloads/files/entire_kiongroup_ar19.pdf, accessed on January 15, 2021 at 10:00 a.m.

KNORR-BREMSE, Annual Report 2019, 2020, available at: https://ir.knorr-bremse.com/download/companies/knorrbremse/Annual%20Reports/DE000KBX1006-JA-2019-EQ-E-00.pdf, accessed on January 15, 2021 at 10:00 a.m.

LANXESS, Annual Report 2019, 2020, available at: https://lanxess.com/-/media/Project/Lanxess/Corporate-Internet/Investors/Publications/Reports/2020/EN/LXS_AR2019_EN_web2.pdf, accessed on January 15, 2021 at 10:00 a.m.

LEG IMMOBILIEN, Annual Report 2019, 2020, available at: https://irpages2.equitystory.com/download/companies/legimmobilien/Annual%20Reports/DE000LEG1110-JA-2019-EQ-E-00.pdf, accessed on January 15, 2021 at 10:00 a.m.

LINDE, Annual Report 2019, 2020, available at: https://investors.linde.com/-/media/linde/investors/documents/full-year-financial-reports/2019-ifrs.pdf?la=en, accessed on January 15, 2021 at 10:00 a.m.

MERCK, Annual Report 2019, 2020, available at: https://www.merckgroup.com/investors/reports-and-financials/earnings-materials/2019-q4/en/2019-Q4-Report-EN.pdf, accessed on January 15, 2021 at 10:00 a.m.

METRO, Annual Report 2018/2019, 2019, available at: https://reports.metroag.de/annual-report/2018-2019/servicepages/downloads/files/entire_metro_ar19.pdf, accessed on January 15, 2021 at 10:00 a.m.

MORPHOSYS, Annual Report 2019, 2020, available at: https://reports.morphosys.com/2019/assets/pdf/mps_gb19_en.pdf, accessed on January 15, 2021 at 10:00 a.m.

MTU AERO ENGINES, Annual Report 2019, 2020, available at: https://www.mtu.de/fileadmin/EN/5_Investor_Relations/7_Financial_Reports/PDFs/2019_Annual_report.pdf, accessed on January 15, 2021 at 10:00 a.m.

MÜNCHENER RÜCK, Annual Report 2019, 2020, available at: https://www.munichre.com/content/dam/munichre/mrwebsiteslaunches/2019-annual-report/MunichRe-Group-Annual-Report-2019-en.pdf/_jcr_content/renditions/original./MunichRe-Group-Annual-Report-2019-en.pdf, accessed on January 15, 2021 at 10:00 a.m.

NEMETSCHEK, Annual Report 2019, 2020, available at: https://ir.nemetschek.com/download/companies/nemetschek/Annual%20Reports/NEM_GB19_Gesamt_en_final_locked.pdf, accessed on January 15, 2021 at 10:15 a.m.

OSRAM LICHT, Annual Report 2019, 2019, available at: https://www.osram-group.com/~/media/Files/O/Osram/Investor%20Relations/Annual%20Report/2019/2019_en_osram_annual_report.pdf, accessed on January 15, 2021 at 10:15 a.m.

PROSIEBENSAT.1 MEDIA, Annual Report 2019, 2020, available at: https://www.prosiebensat1.com/uploads/2020/03/05/P7S1_GB_2019_EN.pdf, accessed on January 15, 2021 at 10:15 a.m.

PUMA, Annual Report 2019, 2020, available at: https://annual-report-2019.puma.com/downloads/puma-ar-2019_annual-report.pdf, accessed on January 15, 2021 at 10:15 a.m.

QIAGEN, Annual Report 2019, 2020, available at: http://financialreport.qiagen.com/sites/default/files/downloads/qiagen_financial_report_complete.pdf, accessed on January 15, 2021 at 10:15 a.m.

RATIONAL, Annual Report 2019, 2020, available at: https://www.rational-online.com/media/investor-relations/annual-reports/rational-annual-report-2019.pdf, accessed on January 15, 2021 at 10:15 a.m.

RHEINMETALL, Annual Report 2019, 2020, available at: https://ir.rheinmetall.com/download/companies/rheinmetall/Annual%20Reports/DE0007030009-JA-2019-EQ-E-01.pdf, accessed on January 15, 2021 at 10:15 a.m.

RWE, Annual Report 2019, 2020, available at: https://www.group.rwe/-/media/RWE/documents/05-investor-relations/2019-Q4/20-03-12-RWE-annual-report-2019.pdf, accessed on January 15, 2021 at 10:15 a.m.

SAP, Annual Report 2019, 2020, available at: https://www.sap.com/docs/download/investors/2019/sap-2019-integrated-report.pdf, accessed on January 15, 2021 at 10:15 a.m.

SARTORIUS, Annual Report 2019, 2020, available at: https://www.sartorius.com/download/404338/16/ssb-annual-report-2019-e-data.pdf, accessed on January 15, 2021 at 10:15 a.m.

SCOUT24, Annual Report 2019, 2020, available at: https://bericht.scout24.com/fileadmin/PDF/Scout24_AR_GroupFinancialReport_2019.pdf, accessed on January 15, 2021 at 10:15 a.m.

SHOP APOTHEKE EUROPE, Annual Report 2019, 2020, available at: https://d1qmdf3vop2l07.cloudfront.net/clover-horse1.cloudvent.net/hash-store/37a8d1c40bf33a0b5ec3b7f53068b6c2.pdf, accessed on January 15, 2021 at 10:15 a.m.

SIEMENS ENERGY, Annual Report 2020, 2020, available at: https://assets.siemens-energy.com/siemens/assets/api/uuid:e28c0ec6-2e23-4dc4-811a-7eccc4bd035f/2020-12-07-siemens-energy-ag-annual-report-2020.pdf, accessed on January 15, 2021 at 10:15 a.m.

SIEMENS HEALTHINEERS, Annual Report 2019, 2019, available at: https://cdn0.scrvt.com/ec41840e14df52192984582863de63fa/1800000006835562/12e08501046c/Siemens-Healthineers-Annual-Report-2019.pdf, accessed on January 15, 2021 at 10:15 a.m.

SIEMENS, Annual Report 2019, 2019, available at: https://assets.new.siemens.com/siemens/assets/api/uuid:0389873c-aed9-444d-9780-4b14b1b7ce57/2019-annual-report.pdf, accessed on January 15, 2021 at 10:15 a.m.

SILTRONIC, Annual Report 2019, 2020, available at: https://www.siltronic.com/fileadmin/investorrelations/2019/Quartal4/Siltronic_Annual_Report_2019_safe.pdf, accessed on January 15, 2021 at 10:30 a.m.

SOFTWARE, Annual Report 2019, 2020, available at: https://investors.softwareag.com/content/dam/investorrelation/pdfs/english/financial-results/2019/q4/200324_en_sow_q4_2019_annual_report.pdf, accessed on January 15, 2021 at 10:30 a.m.

STRÖER, Annual Report 2019, 2020, available at: https://ir.stroeer.com/download/companies/stroeer/Hauptversammlung/12_HV2020_DE0007493991-JA-2019-EQ-E-00.pdf, accessed on January 15, 2021 at 10:30 a.m.

SYMRISE, Annual Report 2019, 2020, available at: https://www.symrise.com/investors/financial-results/index.php?eID=tx_securedownloads&p=1&u=0&g=0&t=1661106572&hash=9b490b0f9524a3a8dae44351d341ea4b2328539a&file=fileadmin/symrise/Downloads_reports/reports/documents/2020/200310_SYM_Financial_Report_2019_.pdf, accessed on January 15, 2021 at 10:30 a.m.

TAG IMMOBILIEN, Annual Report 2019, 2020, available at: https://www.tag-ag.com/fileadmin/content/geschaeftsberichte/TAG-IR-GB2019_ENG_Druckbogen_gesch%C3%BCtzt_neu.pdf, accessed on January 15, 2021 at 10:30 a.m.

TEAMVIEWER, Annual Report 2019, 2020, available at: https://ir.teamviewer.com/download/companies/teamviewer/Annual%20Reports/2020-3-26_TMV_Annual_Report_2019.pdf, accessed on January 15, 2021 at 10:30 a.m.

TELEFONICA DEUTSCHLAND, Annual Report 2019, 2020, available at: https://www.telefonica.de/file/public/1682/TEFD-ANNUAL-REPORT-2019-englisch-online_.pdf?attachment=1, accessed on January 15, 2021 at 10:30 a.m.

THYSSENKRUPP, Annual Report 2018/2019, 2019, available at: https://ucpcdn.thyssenkrupp.com/_legacy/UCPthyssenkruppAG/assets.files/media/investoren/berichterstattung-publikationen/update-21.11.2019/en/thyssenkrupp-gb-2018-2019-en-web_neu.pdf, accessed on January 15, 2021 at 10:30 a.m.

UNIPER, Annual Report 2019, 2020, available at: https://ir.uniper.energy/download/companies/uniperag/Annual%20Reports/DE000UNSE018-JA-2019-EQ-E-00.pdf, accessed on January 15, 2021 at 10:30 a.m.

UNITED INTERNET, Annual Report 2019, 2020, available at: https://www.united-internet.de/fileadmin/publications/United_Internet_Annual_report_2019.pdf, accessed on January 15, 2021 at 10:30 a.m.

VARTA, Annual Report 2019, 2020, available at: https://www.varta-ag.com/fileadmin/varta_ag/publications/financial_and_quarterly_reports/VARTA_AG_GB2019_engl_final.pdf, accessed on January 15, 2021 at 10:30 a.m.

VOLKSWAGEN, Annual Report 2019, 2020, available at: https://www.volkswagenag.com/presence/investorrelation/publications/annual-reports/2020/volkswagen/Y_2019_e.pdf, accessed on January 15, 2021 at 10:30 a.m.

VONOVIA, Annual Report 2019, 2020, available at: https://reports.vonovia.de/2019/annual-report/_assets/downloads/entire_vonovia_ar19.pdf, accessed on January 15, 2021 at 10:30 a.m.

WACKER CHEMIE, Annual Report 2019, 2020, available at: https://reports.wacker.com/2019/annual-report/servicepages/downloads/files/entire_wacker_ar19.pdf, accessed on January 15, 2021 at 10:30 a.m.

ZALANDO, Annual Report 2019, 2020, available at: https://corporate.zalando.com/sites/default/files/media-download/Zalando-SE_Annual-Report_2019.pdf, accessed on January 15, 2021 at 10:30 a.m.

List of Legal Sources of the EC/EU

a) Directives

Directive 2014/56/EU of the European Parliament and of the Council of 16 April 2014 amending Directive 2006/43/EC on statutory audits of annual accounts and consolidated accounts, Official Journal of the European Union L 158 of May 27, 2014, pp. 196–226.

b) Regulations

Commission Regulation (EC) No 1126/2008 of 3 November 2008 adopting certain international accounting standards in accordance with Regulation (EC) No 1606/2002 of the European Parliament and of the Council, Official Journal of the European Union L 320 of November 29, 2008, pp. 1–481.

Commission Regulation (EU) 2018/1595 of 23 October 2018 amending Regulation (EC) No 1126/2008 adopting certain international accounting standards in accordance with Regulation (EC) No 1606/2002 of the European Parliament and of the Council as regards Interpretation 23 of the International Financial Reporting Interpretations Committee, Official Journal of the European Union L 265 of October 24, 2018, pp. 3–8.

Regulation (EC) No 1606/2002 of the European Parliament and of the Council of 19 July 2002 on the application of international accounting standards, Official Journal of the European Communities L 243 of September 11, 2002, pp. 1–4.

c) Conventions

Convention on the elimination of double taxation in connection with the adjustment of profits of associated enterprises (90/463/EEC), Official Journal of the European Communities L 225 of August 20, 1990, pp. 10–24.

List of Laws and Standards

a) German Law and Standards

DRSC, DRSC Interpretations 2021, Berlin 2021.

German Fiscal Code (AO) in the version promulgated on October 1, 2002, Federal Law Gazette I 2002, p. 3866, corrected Federal Law Gazette I 2003, p. 61, last amended by Art. 8 of the Act of February 11, 2021, Federal Law Gazette I 2021, p. 154.

German Code of Administrative Court Procedure (FGO) in the version promulgated on March 28, 2001, Federal Law Gazette I 2001, pp. 442, 2262, corrected Federal Law Gazette I 2002, p. 679, last amended by Art. 7 of the Act of December 12, 2019, Federal Law Gazette I 2019, p. 2633.

German Corporation Tax Act (KStG) in the version promulgated on October 15, 2002, Federal Law Gazette I 2002, p. 4144, last amended by Art. 8 of the Act of December 21, 2020, Federal Law Gazette I 2020, p. 3096.

German Foreign Tax Act (AStG) in the version promulgated on September 8, 1972, Federal Law Gazette I 1972, p. 1713, last amended by Art. 4 of the Act of March 25, 2019, Federal Law Gazette I 2019, p. 357.

German Commercial Code (HGB) in the version promulgated on May 10, 1897, Reich Law Gazette I 1897, p. 219, last amended by Art. 14 of the Act of December 22, 2020, Federal Law Gazette I 2020, p. 3256.

b) US Law and Standards

Financial Accounting Foundation, Accounting Standards Codification 2021, Norwalk 2021.

Financial Accounting Foundation, Statement of Financial Accounting Standards 2021, Norwalk 2021.

Financial Accounting Foundation, FASB Interpretations 2021, Norwalk 2021.

c) International Law and Standards

IFRS Foundation, IFRS Standards 2021, London 2021.

IFRS Foundation, IFRIC Interpretations 2021, London 2021.

List of Jurisprudence

BFH, Judgement of October 19, 1993, VIII R 14/92, Federal Law Gazette II 1993, pp. 891–893.

List of Administrative Instructions

a) Administrative Instructions

BMF, Letter of July 24, 2015, IV C 2 – S 2750-a/07/10002, in: Federal Law Gazette I 2015, pp. 612–613.

b) Decrees

German Fiscal Code Application Decree (AEAO) of January 31, 2014, Federal Law Gazette I 2014, p. 290, last amended by BMF letter of January 28, 2021, Federal Law Gazette I 2021, pp. 145–146.

The manufacturer's authorised representative in the EU is Springer Nature Customer Service Centre GmbH, Europaplatz 3, 69115 Heidelberg, Germany. If you have any concerns regarding our products, please contact ProductSafety@springernature.com

Printed and bound by CPI Group (UK) Ltd, Croydon, CR0 4YY
28/09/2026
02224076-0005